In all forms of leadership, whether you are a coach, a CEO, or a parent, there are four words that, when said, can bring out the best in your team, your employees, and your family.

I BELIEVE IN YOU.

Those four words can mean the difference between a fear of failure and the courage to try.

—Coach K

"On the court and off, Krzyzewski is a family man first, a teacher second, a basketball coach third, and a winner at all three. He is what is right about sports."

—*The Sporting News*

"You can mix unlimited academic expectations with unlimited winning. That's what Coach K has proven at Duke."

—*USA Today*

ALSO BY MIKE KRZYZEWSKI

Five-Point Play
Leading with the Heart

BEYOND BASKETBALL

COACH K'S KEYWORDS FOR SUCCESS

MIKE KRZYZEWSKI

with JAMIE K. SPATOLA

GRAND
CENTRAL

NEW YORK   BOSTON

Grand Central Publishing
Hachette Book Group
1290 Avenue of the Americas, New York, NY 10104
grandcentralpublishing.com
twitter.com/grandcentralpub

Originally published in hardcover and ebook by Grand Central Publishing in October 2006
First Trade Paperback Edition: October 2007
Reissued: March 2023

Grand Central Publishing is a division of Hachette Book Group, Inc. The Grand Central Publishing name and logo is a trademark of Hachette Book Group, Inc.

The publisher is not responsible for websites (or their content) that are not owned by the publisher.

The Hachette Speakers Bureau provides a wide range of authors for speaking events. To find out more, go to hachettespeakersbureau.com or email HachetteSpeakers@hbgusa.com.

Grand Central Publishing books may be purchased in bulk for business, educational, or promotional use. For information, please contact your local bookseller or the Hachette Book Group Special Markets Department at special.markets@hbgusa.com.

Library of Congress Control Number: 2006928991

ISBN: 9780446580496 (hardcover), 9780759516748 (ebook),
9780446581875 (trade paperback), 9781538741603 (trade paperback reissue)

Printed in the United States of America

LSC

Printing 3, 2023

Dedicated to Captain Chris Spatola, who goes above and beyond in so many ways.
—M.K. and J.K.S.

ACKNOWLEDGMENT

Intimate experiences are precious in life. I have enjoyed one of the most intimate in writing this book with my daughter Jamie. We have spent a lot of time together on airplanes, in gyms, sharing meals, talking on the phone, and I have loved every second of it.

Since she was a little girl, Jamie has loved to write and I have known that she has a gift. I have used her gift to help me share some of my life stories with you and she made it easy for me. I often say that two is better than one if two can act as one. Jamie and I truly acted as one and grew together during this project. I thank her as I love her—with all of my heart.

—Mike Krzyzewski
June 2006

CONTENTS

INTRODUCTION

I am a believer in the power of words.

Before many of our team's practices and games, I will write a single word or two on the whiteboard of our locker room. To me, these solitary words speak more than any lengthy speech. I want to have each player picture himself doing these words: having *passion*, striving for *excellence*, playing with *poise*. When my players take the court and momentarily lose sight of our team's goal for that game, they can think back on that one word. They regain focus and they can look around at their teammates and know that that word resonates in their minds as well. They may even repeat that word in a huddle, or I may say it on the bench during one of our time-outs. It keeps us together and committed to a common goal, even in the heat of the game.

When you read this book, I want you to ask

yourself an important question: how do our brains assign meaning to a particular word? Many of you would respond by reciting a dictionary definition: what the word signifies, its pronunciation, its etymology, and what it means to us today. If you have a good dictionary, you may even be offered the word in the context of a sentence. The dictionary is a great thing to study if you want to learn how to use words in sentences, paragraphs, in speeches and novels. Remember, however, that you are only borrowing these words.

This book is not about merely USING or BORROWING words; it is about OWNING them.

To incorporate these words into your own life, or to teach them to your own team, your business, or your children, merely memorizing a definition is insufficient. Anyone, through enough practice and repetition, can recite the definitions to countless words. But for these words to become instinct, part of the person you are, requires understanding.

So, in addition to an explanation of meaning, I would like to offer you a story from my own life to accompany each word. For me, these stories encapsulate not only a definition but a moment in my life in which the word's true meaning became abundantly clear. I want you to imagine yourself in those stories and try to get a grasp of how that word played a key role in my life, the life of my family or my teams. I am honored to lend you our stories.

But my ultimate goal in writing this book is for you to have your own stories, for you to look into your past and pay attention to your present so that your image of the word will become a story from your own life experiences. I truly feel that we all should be able to write this book.

Then, when your son or daughter, your player or employee asks you what the word means, you won't recite them a definition; you will tell them a story. When you talk about life's most vital and beautiful words, you are not merely borrowing them from a dictionary or from someone else's life experiences, they are yours. Those words belong to you.

I hope that you find these words as powerful as I do, that you will believe in them, and, most of all, that they become your own.

BEYOND BASKETBALL

Adaptability

As a point guard at West Point, I had the privilege of playing for the legendary Bob Knight, a tough coach and probably the best of all time. There was one particular drill, called "Zig Zag," that we did in practice every single day. It was a defensive drill that was difficult and physically exhausting. Though it's a great and effective drill, my teammates and I dreaded it, but we always knew it was coming.

Five years later, after the completion of my service in the United States Army, I was able to reunite with Coach Knight as a graduate assistant coach at Indiana for the 1974–75 season. It was an unbelievable start for a coaching career, because not only did I have the opportunity to work under the best in the business, but he also had the number one team in the country that year with such standout players as Scott May, Kent Benson, and Quinn Buckner.

At our very first practice of the season, I was so excited just to be there. But I couldn't help but notice that we did not do the "Zig Zag" drill. In the locker room after practice, I was thinking about saying something to Coach Knight about it, but I thought better of it, and didn't say anything. Surely we would do the drill tomorrow.

The next day, we had a great practice, but again, no "Zig Zag." That day, Coach Knight seemed like he was in a pretty good mood and I was feeling sure of myself.

"Coach," I said, to get his attention.

"What?" he responded. I was already thinking that this was a mistake, but at this point I had to say it.

"Well, at Army, we did the 'Zig Zag' drill every single day, often multiple times. How come we haven't done it with this team?"

Coach Knight walked calmly over to me, put his hand on my shoulder, and said, "Michael, there is a big difference between you and Quinn Buckner."

He was right. Drills like "Zig Zag" that are a necessity for some teams may not be appropriate for others. You have to adapt what you do based on who you are. A drill that Mike Krzyzewski needs to do every day, Quinn Buckner may never have to do or may only have to do infrequently. Every player is different, every team is different, and to merely apply a formula is not fair to those players or those teams.

You can always learn something from great teachers. I had the privilege to learn from one of the best coaches of all time. From Coach Knight, I learned passion, commitment, persistence, and intensity. But I also learned adaptability.

That lesson is the reason why I have written a different practice plan for every single practice of my career. In teaching, you must remember that no group or individual is the same as who you taught the day before, the year before, or the decade before. Your plan has to suit who you and your team are *right now*. And you must always be willing to adapt. When you do, you and your team will be even more successful.

Adversity

What I believe separates good teams and individuals from great ones is the manner in which they handle adversity. Do you let it beat you or do you use it to make you better?

Adversity can teach you more about yourself than any success, and overcoming an obstacle can sometimes feel even better than achieving an easy victory. Additionally, you can discover things about your endurance, your ability to turn a negative into a positive, and your personal strength of heart.

One of the greatest comments I ever heard about adversity came from the current Duke University president, Richard Brodhead. He said to me, "You outlive your darkest day." In other words, failure can never be your destination. In adverse circumstances, you must remind yourself that this day is not your last. You will get through it, but can you use it to get better? Improvement comes as the result of adversity; it comes from learning about limits and how to break those limits. Whenever I face adversity, I look *at* the problem and then *beyond* the problem. I look for the solution and then I look for the positive impact it will have on me, my team, or my family.

In the summer of 2003, after doing a speaking engagement in Colorado Springs, I heard on television the frightening news that my former Duke point guard Jason Williams had been in a horrific motorcycle accident. I immediately made calls to find out about Jason and learned that he was in serious condition and had been taken to a trauma center in Chicago. The initial prognosis was that he had a chance of losing his leg and never being able to walk again. I immediately changed my original schedule and flew to Chicago to be with him.

On the flight, I thought about Jason's current condition and all that he had already accomplished in his young life: he was a Duke University graduate, a National Champion, a two-time National Player of the Year, and he had his jersey retired and hanging from the rafters in Cameron Indoor Stadium.

One thing that had always blown me away about Jason is that he was never afraid to make mistakes. In the 2001 National Championship game, Jason had hit only one three-pointer in ten attempts, but going into the last few minutes of the game, I called a play for him to shoot another three. He was not afraid to take that next shot. And he hit the three that proved to be the biggest shot in the last few minutes of the game. As a result, we all became National Champions. Jason was fearless because he grew up with great parents, knowing that he had their unconditional love and support and that a mistake was never the end-all. I tried to offer him the same type of support during his college career. His fearlessness made him one of the best players I have ever coached.

I will always remember walking into Jason's hospital room, seeing him in that condition, and hugging his crying mother and father. As I bent over and kissed him on his forehead, Jason said to me, "Coach, thanks for being here."

I then proceeded to talk to Jason in positive terms about the fact that he would not only walk again but also would be in the NBA again. I gave him a holy saint's medal of mine that I had carried with me for years. Every time he looked at the medal, I wanted him to look beyond the adversity he was currently facing and to remember that those who love him will be behind him throughout his recovery and the rest of his life. I wanted to give him *a destination beyond the devastation*. I said to him,

"Jason, this medal is very special to me, but I want to lend it to you. You have to promise to give it back to me the day that you play in your next NBA game. And you can be sure that I will be there." The doctors would talk about the solution to Jason's medical problems, but I wanted to be sure that, mentally and emotionally, he was looking beyond the problem and that his destination was not adversity, but success.

I have always known that Jason has the heart of a champion and with him it is best to let him follow his instincts. Winners expect to win. And Jason expects that he will come out a champion yet again. His limits have been tested in a very serious way. But he is approaching this scary situation and his arduous recovery with the same fearlessness with which he played every game of basketball. He has taken his recovery time to develop as a student of the game, attending as many games as possible, asking questions of other players and coaches, and even doing television commentary during some games. Because I know Jason has a winner's heart, it doesn't surprise me to watch as he has gone from not knowing whether or not he will walk again to having the opportunity to begin playing basketball.

The adversity did not beat him. Rather, he has used it as an opportunity to grow as a person and to learn a great deal about what a strong man he is, mentally, emotionally, and physically. Jason looked at his adversity and beyond, and his champion heart has him running and jumping again, less than three years later. What a winner!

Balance

Drive, passion, and intensity: these are all good things. They are elemental to finding success in your life and career. But just as important to life as all of these things is balance. Being motivated in your career is important, but you must be cautious not to become one-dimensional. If there is no balance between the time and energy spent on your career, your family, your religion, your friendships, and community service, you can become unbalanced internally.

I was reminded of the need for balance by my then eleven-year-old daughter, Jamie, after a heartbreaking loss in 1993. Our team had won back-to-back NCAA National Championships in 1991 and 1992, but California had just beaten us to end our pursuit of a third title in a row.

On the jet going back to North Carolina that

night, the mood was very somber. I walked down the aisle of the plane thanking our cheerleaders and band members for all that they had done as a part of our team. At the same time, I was watching my players, and particularly my seniors, to see if any of them needed my friendship or assistance during this difficult time. I heard Jamie's voice whispering, "Dad, come here." At first I tried not to pay attention to her because I was focused on my team. But she was persistent. When I went over to her, she said, "Dad, can we have a family meeting tomorrow?"

We had not had a family meeting in a number of months, and there I was, worried about my team, and my eleven-year-old wanted to call one. However, always wanting to give my children the time and attention they deserve, I agreed to a meeting the next evening at six o'clock.

That next morning, Jamie came into our bedroom with clipboard and pen in hand. She asked me to rank my level of happiness on a scale of one to five: one being the lowest, and five being the highest. Because of the loss and the mood I was in, I wanted to tell her it was a zero. But, because she was eleven, I told her it was a three: a very mediocre response.

"Okay," she said, taking note of my answer, "now, how would you rate your happiness level if we were to get a dog?"

I could see where this was going but I responded anyway. "Four."

At 6:00 p.m. sharp, we all gathered in the family room. Jamie had the entire family in front of
her, and behind her two posters. The first sign
read, in large letters, "Issue #1: A Dog," and below
it had the action statement, "Act Now." Next to it,
the second sign read, "Issue #2: Family Vacation,"
and below that, "Badly Needed." With a pointer,
she indicated the first topic and began to plead her
case. She even revealed a bar graph she had drawn
displaying the family level of happiness without a
dog and the projected level of happiness should we
decide to get a family pet. The graph showed that
the family happiness level would go from 60 percent to 80 percent. A shocking 20 percent increase
in overall family happiness! She then used her
pointer to indicate the action statement as she read
aloud the words, "Act Now."

During the next twenty minutes, the discussion
turned into the typical family debate over whether
or not to get a pet. Who would train the puppy?
Who would take the time to walk and exercise him?
Who would clean up his messes? After the uncon-
vincing responses that my daughters would take
care of all of those things, we told Jamie that it was
not going to happen. Jamie cried. The meeting was
over. We never even got to issue number two.

The next day I left for a recruiting trip. When I
returned the following day, I opened the door, and
to my surprise, we had a dog: a beautiful black Lab
puppy that we named Defense. In that situation, Jamie proved to be wrong. She
said the happiness would increase by 20 percent; it
actually went up 40 percent, because now we were
100 percent happy. Defense turned out to be an
amazing addition. And, a year later, we added another dog to our family, a chocolate Lab named
Cameron. "D" and "Cammy" have brought joy,
comfort, and unconditional love into our everyday
lives. When I come home from a long trip or a hard
practice, there is nothing I love to do more than
get down on the floor and spend time with our
dogs.

After getting to know Defense for a couple of
days, I left town again to work for CBS during the
1993 Final Four. I was gone for seven days. When I
returned home, I was exhausted and emotionally
drained but was scheduled to leave the next day for
a five-day recruiting trip. As I was sitting in the family room, I looked up and Jamie's signs were still
there. I stared hard at the sign that read, "Family
Vacation: Badly Needed." After thinking momentarily, I canceled the recruiting trip and took that
time to go to the beach with my family.

While at the beach, I was able to spend some

one-on-one time with my middle daughter, Lindy, who was going through a very difficult teenage crisis. After a long walk on the beach and a great discussion, we together had come up with a solution to the crisis. Our family happiness increased yet again. All because my eleven-year-old daughter persisted in making sure that I keep balance in my life. As a leader and a career-oriented individual, you must take care not to allow one aspect of your life to so consume you that you neglect the others. Your family and friends are there to remind you when you need to "act now" on regaining some balance and when getting back on the right and healthy track is "badly needed." At a time in my life when my career had stirred up some very intense emotions, I was reminded to put time into the other parts of my life, and it ended up changing all of us for the better. Balance can put things in perspective, can bring you joy even when you are down, and can allow you to be at your best in all aspects of your life.

Belief

Those three magic words "I love you" are words that are important and meaningful in any culture. But there are four words that are not said nearly enough by families interacting with kids or people interacting in a team environment.

In all forms of leadership, whether you are a coach, a CEO, or a parent, there are four words that, when said, can bring out the best in your team, your employees, and your family.

"I believe in you."

Those four words can mean the difference between a fear of failure and the courage to try. When you look someone in the eyes and tell them, "I believe in you," you are letting them know, "You are not going to take this journey alone. I'm not going to allow you to." When someone believes in you, it helps you to overcome the anxiety that comes as a result of feeling alone. Belief raises your confidence level and allows you to try things that are impossible to do by yourself.

On a team or in a family, belief makes each individual stronger and also fortifies the group as a whole. You know that there is somebody there to catch you if you fall, and someone to give you that extra push when you need it to overcome an obstacle.

When a group shares belief you share the brunt of any defeat, making it easier to turn a mistake into a positive. Likewise, successes feel even better because you share the rewards. You have all been a part of the success. In an atmosphere of belief, both wins and losses are shared.

Belief does not occur naturally; you have to work for it, earn it, and continue to deserve it. The basis of belief is in individual relationships. If I lie to you, I create a breach in that relationship, and it becomes more difficult for you to believe what I say. As powerful as belief can make you and your team, it is also fragile. You have to take care of it.

BELIEF IN ACTION

When I think about belief, the first person that comes to mind is my associate head coach, Johnny Dawkins. My first couple of years at Duke were difficult times. In two seasons, I had a 27–30 record, and many critics were anxious to see me fired. In our first couple of seasons, my staff and I had tried to recruit a large number of kids and had fallen short on most of them; we had cast our net too wide. So we changed our strategy. We decided that we were going to be much more focused in our recruiting effort, giving us a chance to form meaningful relationships with the few kids we were trying to bring in.

Johnny Dawkins was a highly touted high school standout from Washington, D.C. I can remember spending time with him and his family in the living room of their home and I remember his spending time with my family at ours. My four-year-old daughter, Lindy, even handed him a note asking him if he was coming to Duke, providing "yes" and "no" boxes for him to check. Johnny and I bonded instantly. I knew he was something special.

Recruiting in those days was more difficult for me because I had no résumé to show. I didn't have a winning record and we had not won any championships. So, in recruiting Johnny Dawkins, who was being pursued by all of the top schools, I was really asking him to believe in me, even though I didn't have any tangible reasons to offer as to why he should.

He was our first major recruit, our first major talent, and our first McDonald's All-America. I can never emphasize enough what Johnny's commitment to me and to Duke meant to our future success. As much as a great player needs a start, needs someone to believe in his ability, a coach needs a start too. I did not always win at Duke. There was a time when we were nowhere near the top of the college basketball ranks. *I needed someone to believe in me. Johnny did that and I am so thankful that he did.*

After coming to Duke and having an incredible career, scoring more than 2,500 points and being named National Player of the Year, Johnny was a lottery pick in the draft and had a long and successful career in the NBA. And, as much as Johnny showed belief in me, I always believed in him as well. If he missed four or five shots in a row, I would remind him to keep shooting, to treat every shot like it was his first. Because we both exhibited mutual belief, we developed an amazing bond as a coach and a player. Following the example set by him, we have continued to have success in recruiting some of the top high school players.

As if he hadn't already done enough, Johnny came back to Duke as a coach, and our bond continued to develop as head coach and associate head coach. And there is no one more qualified to pass on our shared belief to others than Johnny Dawkins, whose power to believe got this whole thing started.

Johnny was a trailblazer. His commitment to Duke and our mutual belief stands as the foundation of the tradition we have established for our program: a foundation of strong belief. My assistants and I continue to go into the living rooms of talented young men and tell them that we believe in them and ask if they, too, will believe in us. And, thanks to Johnny Dawkins, the example has been set. When those youngsters agree to believe in us and we commit to believing in them, great teams, players, and traditions are born.

Care

When you care about someone or something you show genuine concern for that person or thing, in good times and bad.

In the development of our basketball teams, care is as crucial an aspect as any. You want to care about one another as individuals, have empathy and compassion. And you also want to care about each other's performances on the court. When you care about one another *and* about your purpose, you are compelled to put your feelings into action.

Care is so important to a team because, if you want to change limits, there are going to be times when members of the team make mistakes. When you make a mistake, and you know it, you become very vulnerable. The immediate responses of those on your team, those you trust the most, will determine how you perceive your mistake. It can make you feel fearful of making that mistake again. Or you can feel that you put yourself on the line, and even though you did not succeed, you know that your teammates care about you and you will not hesitate to step up again. You never want to let a mistake be the last time an individual dares to try. Care makes you more confident. You know that you have someone's unconditional support. It creates an atmosphere that breeds success and gives you the confidence to try again.

Care is developed by fostering individual relationships. This means not only caring about how the team does on the basketball court but caring about their lives off the court and taking the time to get to know who they really are as a person, not only as a basketball player. Several times a year, my wife, Mickie, and I will have the team over to the house for an afternoon. We will serve a casual meal, put football games on the television, and allow the guys to relax and be themselves. Additionally, I will often meet with the players one-on-one and ask them questions about their lives: their families, their girlfriends, their classes. These are all opportunities to show my team that they are not merely basketball players to me. I genuinely care for each and every one of them, and after our time together while they are at Duke, I will continue to care about them. I absolutely love when my former players call me to ask for my input or advice, or even just to catch up. It is the ultimate proof that I have been successful in showing that I do care for them.

CARE IN ACTION

After our 1999 season in which we played in the National Championship game, I was at home recuperating from hip replacement surgery. Our great player and leader Trajan Langdon had graduated, and three of our players had decided to leave the program early to pursue a career in the NBA. One player transferred to another school. From a team that was one of the best in the nation and won 37 games, we now had only three veteran players returning. In many ways, I began to feel down and alone. Chris Carrawell, Nate James, and Shane Battier, who would become our team captains for the following season, came to visit me. They set up three chairs next to my bed and we sat there and had a long discussion about what was to come. The first thing they said to me was, "Coach, how are you doing?" Such a simple question but, for me, it carried so much meaning. They were asking how I was doing after my operation but also how I was doing in coping with the loss of so much of the team. My answer was a completely honest one. "I am okay now that you guys are here."

These three guys had taken the initiative to

come to my house and show me that they cared. While I was experiencing much doubt about the upcoming season, this meeting revived me. By the time they left, we were all talking about where we were headed that year, and because they had shown such care for me, I was able to tell them confidently that I thought we were going to have a great team and a great season. I looked at them and said that we were going to be good and then asked them, "Do you believe it?"

The response I received from Chris Carrawell is one of the greatest things a player has ever said to me. He said, *"Coach, if you say it, I believe it."*

The next season, we finished 29–5 overall, were ACC regular season champions with a 15–1 record, and ACC Tournament champions. The following year, Shane Battier and Nate James were leaders on our 2001 National Championship team. After a difficult time for me and the Duke program, those three players showed me that they truly cared. It gave me the foundation of support I needed to move on positively and develop my team to the highest level. All because they cared.

Challenges

After meeting with some success, it is often difficult for a leader to maintain a high level of passion. One way to avoid getting into a rut is to ensure that you are not doing the same thing over and over each year. I try to see each season as a new challenge because I have a new team to work with, new opponents to encounter, and often new ideas and theories to try. Approaching each season in this manner helps keep me fresh.

I think it is important not to get into a personal comfort zone. To avoid this, I try to constantly take on new challenges, to test limits, and, often, to discover that those limits were never really there. Approaching the same challenges with fresh eyes and taking on entirely new challenges isn't easy, but it can help you discover things about yourself that you may have never known, even at fifty-nine years old!

Over recent years, I have taken on such challenges as motivational speaking, the building of the
Emily Krzyzewski Family Life Center, and an XM
Satellite Radio show. And in the fall of 2005 I accepted one of the greatest challenges of my career.

It was a great honor when Jerry Colangelo,
managing director of USA Basketball, offered me
the position of United States National Team coach
for three years, culminating with the 2008 Summer
Olympics in Beijing. However, there were some
personal issues within my family that needed to be
discussed before I accepted the honor. My wife,
daughters, and their husbands, while realizing the
magnitude of this opportunity, were concerned
that such a large undertaking would make my already busy schedule simply impossible. Additionally, they brought up health concerns that often
accompany being overworked and exhausted: legit-
imate concerns, considering that sickness and ex-
haustion kept me from coaching my team the
second half of the season in 1994–95.

At a dinner with my entire family, each raised
their worries about the undertaking, and the discussion was at times contentious and emotional.
But I explained how I feel about challenges, how
they keep me fresh, young, and hungry. When
everyone understood that I saw this position as an
incredible honor, a chance to serve our great coun-

try, and a new personal challenge, they all took a deep breath and understood. When approaching new challenges, it is imperative that you have the support of those who love you most. Now that I know their support is there, I can throw myself into this experience knowing that, even if I fail, my family will have my back.

No matter how successful you believe yourself to be, you can never feel as if you've reached the absolute pinnacle. There are always new and wonderful challenges out there, and part of maintaining success is knowing when you need to accept them. I am rejuvenated, I am nervous, I am eager, and I am so excited to discover what amazing things I will learn as a result of taking on this new challenge.

Collective Responsibility

We win and we lose together.

The best way I can describe collective responsibility is to point to a scoreboard. At any point in the game, when you look up there, there is no one individual's name. Instead, it shows the team name: Duke, the Chicago Bulls, the USA. This means that in no way does a single individual win or lose a game. Each game, and indeed each moment within a game, is the responsibility of the entire team.

On a team that wins and loses together, there is no such thing as blame. Blame is a destructive force within a group and has no place in the locker room of a true team. *When somebody does something well, we all do it well. When somebody makes a mistake, we all make the mistake.* Outsiders, like opposing fans and the media, can say what they will: Christian's missed free throws lost the game for Duke, or Sean's last-second three-pointer is the reason we won. But behind closed doors, we know beyond any doubt that this is not true. If we won, we did it together. If we lost, that responsibility belongs to all of us as well.

Handling the responsibility for wins and losses together removes the burden from one individual's shoulders and distributes it among each member of the team. Sometimes a load is too heavy for one to carry alone. Just imagine: *what could you do if you believed you could not fail?* Being on a team that embraces collective responsibility puts you in that position. You, individually, cannot fail. That atmosphere is conducive to high-level performance and places you and your team in the position to be bold and unafraid, and if you should lose, you are not alone.

One concept I have always tried to instill in my teams is the idea that you play for the name on the front of your jersey and not the name on the back. In other words, you play as a member of the Duke team, not for the name that appears across the back of your jersey. When your team embraces that concept, then *we* competed in a game and *we* either won or lost.

J.J. Redick is the all-time leading scorer in Duke Basketball history, the leading scorer in Atlantic Coast Conference history, and the NCAA's leader in three-point shooting. He was a great player for us, the National Player of the Year. In our 2005–06 season, the media focused an incredible amount of attention on the young man, tracing how many points he needed to hit his next milestone, praising him when he had scored 30 or more points in 14 games (a Duke record), and chastising him when he had an off shooting night.

Because of the incredible amount of personal pressure placed on J.J. to score points for us and the added pressure of chasing and breaking so many records, it was often difficult for him to remember that the fate of our team and our season did not rest squarely on his shoulders.

In J.J.'s final game at Duke, we played Louisiana State University in the Sweet Sixteen. He had his worst game of the season, going 3 for 18 shooting. We lost. When J.J. came out of the game with nine seconds left, he was completely distraught. In his own mind, he took full responsibility for the loss and knew that there would not be another game to make amends. His teammates and coaches tried to console him, but it was to no avail. It really took a couple of weeks before J.J. was able to believe that it was not his fault. We had to remind him that if it were not for his performance throughout the season, we never would have been in the Sweet Sixteen. J.J. had allowed our entire team to take collective responsibility for all 32 of our wins dur-

COLLECTIVE RESPONSIBILITY 29

ing the season, and this time he needed to allow us, as his teammates, to help take responsibility for the LSU loss.

Earlier in the season, J.J. was able to pass the lesson of collective responsibility on to one of the younger members of our team. He embraced being a part of a team and, though he was very hard on himself, he knew the importance of collective responsibility. Our first loss of the season was to Georgetown in late January by a narrow three-point margin. With six and a half seconds left on the clock, we had a chance to tie, but our freshman point guard, Greg Paulus, dribbled into a bad situation and was unable to get the ball to J.J. for a shot. When the buzzer sounded, J.J. walked off the court with his arm around Greg. "I told him it's okay," he said afterward. *"We win together, we lose together."* Moments like that make me proud to be a coach.

J.J.'s reaffirmation of our team philosophy of collective responsibility was a reminder to Greg that his play did not decide the game for us. We lost that one together. But because we all maintained responsibility, we were able to win many more games together, finishing with a 32–4 record and becoming both the outright ACC regular season and ACC Tournament champions. We were collectively responsible for a great season.

Commitment

Aside from the vows I took with my wife, Mickie, thirty-seven years ago, the most life-altering commitment of my life came from my first athletic director at Duke, Tom Butters.

In 2004, representatives from the Los Angeles Lakers came into my living room and offered me $40 million to become their coach. In the days that followed, my family and I did our best to evaluate who we were and where we were going. In that time of self-analysis, I called my former AD.

"Mike, what are you calling me for?" he asked, surprised to hear my voice.

"Well, whenever I need good advice, I always come to you. And right now I need some good advice. Tom, someone just came into my house and offered me $40 million to coach their team. Now, when I first signed on at Duke in 1980, my starting salary was $40,000. We've come a long way since then."

Tom jokingly replied, "Well, I think I deserve a 10 percent finder's fee."

"Sounds fair," I responded. "I'll send you a check for $4,000!"

We both laughed and enjoyed the moment before delving into the more serious aspects of my situation. When it comes time to make important decisions, I always seek Tom's advice. His commitment to me, even after my first three seasons with a 38–47 record, is why I was able to get things going at Duke. I never doubted his support. And because he was committed to me and never doubted me, *I never doubted me.* His commitment made me better because I was never afraid of losing my job. It is easy to be committed to someone or something during good times, because when you are winning, your commitment is never challenged. But loyalty and dedication during more difficult times can be tough. Tom never wavered, and when commitment doesn't waver, that's when you have the greatest chance of winning. And we did win!

During the seventeen years that he was my boss, he always told me to follow my instincts. Even when we had losing records, he never interfered, he only asked me that I ensure our student-athletes were a good representation of Duke both on and off the court.

When I think back on his decision to hire me, I am amazed. He told me years later, that, following my job interview in 1980, he simply couldn't get me out of his mind. He tried to convince himself that I was not the right one for the job. But when it came down to it, he just had to follow his heart. From that day forward, we were on the same team.

Tom gave me the same advice on that summer day in 2004 that he always had. He told me to be myself, to make sure that I continue to do what I love, and to follow my instincts. The decision became easy. Because of Tom's commitment to me, I developed a commitment to Duke that I knew I could never give up. Not only that, but he taught me to be committed to myself and to follow my heart. As long as I am coaching, I will give my Duke teams the very same commitment that Tom Butters gave me.

Communication

Lffective teamwork begins and ends with communication. The word, of course, means to convey a message. In order to communicate with your teammates, coworkers, or family, you must ask yourself and one another two critical questions:

- How do we talk to one another?
- How do we listen?

However, communication does not always occur naturally, even among a tight-knit group of individuals. Communication must be *taught* and *practiced* in order to bring everyone together as one.

My team has one rule regarding communication: *when you talk to one another, you look each other in the eye.* Eye contact is an important act of mutual respect but also enforces the most crucial element of communicating: telling the truth. Lying and quibbling are unnecessary impediments to working as a team. Face-to-face communication and truth should serve as the basis of all team communication. In our team's preparation, there are three systems that I and my coaching staff try to instill. Of course, there is an offensive system and a defensive system consisting of basketball "x's and o's," but there is also a communication system. In our locker room conversations, tape sessions, and individual meetings, I encourage my players to look me in the eye and to be honest and forthright, never feeling afraid to express themselves. In these meetings we establish a system of communication steeped in honesty. By eliminating counterproductive quibbling, we establish our basis for collective communication among all members of the team, top to bottom.

On the basketball court, there is very little time to get your message across. In the heat of a game, a basketball team speaks a different language; it is not a language based on long sentences, but it is a language nonetheless. To acclimate our team to speaking this language, we do not merely drill defensive stances and positioning in our practices, we drill talking. When you talk, your body reacts, your hands get ready, and your mind becomes prepared to respond, even under pressure.

On our Duke Basketball teams, I never want to be the only communicator. In order for a message to get across, it must be echoed by every member of the group. I constantly look for members of my team who can help convey the message. It starts with my staff. Currently my coaching staff consists of three of my former players. I like having my former players as assistants because they have already been a part of the culture we instill in our young men. Often my assistants are better equipped to communicate a particular message to the team because they can present the same message in their own words or provide more current examples. It is difficult for me to believe that I am now forty years older than my players—I never thought I'd be forty years older than anybody! So my staff often helps to bridge the communication gap that can exist between generations.

The bottom line on communication is that everyone on a team should feel comfortable expressing themselves. The freedom to express oneself to other members of a team, business, or family breeds a sense of ownership. And, most importantly, each member of the team knows that when we look each other in the eye and communicate, we are honest. That type of communication can help to turn a group of individuals into a true team.

COMMUNICATION IN ACTION

I remember a few years ago I gave my team a motivational speech in our locker room before practice. At the time, I thought it was a great speech, one that would surely inspire an energetic and passionate practice. So as we left the locker room to take the court, I was proud of myself. I thought to myself, as far as speeches go, there's King, there's Lincoln, and there's me. But as we stepped onto the court, there was no pat on the back from my assistants or surge of excitement from the team. They calmly jogged out on the court and not a word was spoken.

As we took the court for practice, I asked my assistants, searching for a compliment, "How do you think it went?" Instead of the praise I had expected, my assistant Steve Wojciechowski said to me, "Coach, I don't think they understood anything you said." At first I was angry with that response because it was not what I expected. However, it was honest and made me realize that my message did not get across to my team.

I asked the team to come and sit on the bleachers and listen. When they were all gathered in front of me I asked if they had understood what I said to them in the locker room. Shane Battier, one of our team captains, stepped up and said, "No, Coach, we didn't understand."

"Well, here's what I was trying to say." I proceeded to sum up in about thirty seconds the message that I had previously tried to convey in a fifteen-minute speech. I then told Shane that if that ever happened again, I needed to know right away that my message was not received. I needed immediate communication. Shane said, "I got it, Coach. Let's start practice."

That is the type of communication I want on my team, the type where everybody can express themselves and no one feels stifled. I want the type of communication where, even if your head coach believes he has delivered the basketball equivalent of the Gettysburg Address, you can tell him that his message has not resonated. That rare but essential brand of communication turns a group of individuals with different backgrounds, talents, and ideas into a unit that can effectively talk and listen, both on and off the court.

Courage

I often share with my Duke Basketball teams a Winston Churchill quote: *"Courage is the first of human qualities because it is the quality which guarantees all the others."*

In other words, you can possess countless good qualities as an individual, but if you don't have the courage to proceed, you may never see those qualities come to fruition. It takes courage to put what you believe to be the best of you on the line, to test it, and to see how far it takes you. Courage means daring to do what you imagine.

For the most part, people do not attempt things because they fear the consequences. But the greatest consequence of all comes in not attempting to do the things that you believe you can. Having courage means boldly pursuing your dreams, no matter what the consequences may be.

Sometimes in basketball games, I will bring my players into a huddle and see fear in their eyes. Maybe a particular player has missed several shots in a row, or perhaps the opposing team has made a run and put us back on our heels. My job as a leader is to show them a face of courage. That is what a team is all about. When one individual gets down or afraid, they will look to their teammates and their leader, in particular, to bring them out of it. I want my face to tell them, "Let's all get together and let's do those things that we imagined and prepared for in practice. Let's have the courage to do the actions necessary to reach our goals." I want to take them past the hurdle of fear and help them in times of both individual and collective doubt. All of a sudden, we walk away from that huddle and, together, we are going to go after it. We are going to have a chance.

I can remember a time of extreme doubt in my life when I was offered the chance to attend the United States Military Academy and to play basketball there. At first there was no way I was going to go. I was too afraid and too full of self-doubt. But I received the encouragement I needed from my parents, my greatest supporters.

My father, in particular, was not a man of many words, but when it came to ensuring that his son did not turn down a great opportunity because of simple fear, he was vocal and emphatic. Thanks to him and my mom, I was able to find the inner courage to make the right decision, one that shaped who I would become as an adult. Just look at the word "encouragement" and you will see that it means helping another find courage. *Always surround yourself with individuals who will help to enable your courage when it is lacking from within.*

The most courageous player I ever coached was Bobby Hurley. Even when I myself felt stifled by moments of doubt, I could look into Bobby's eyes and find the confidence to proceed. My job in coaching him was to give him the freedom to boldly follow his instincts.

In the 1991 NCAA semifinal game against the University of Nevada–Las Vegas, we were a considerable underdog. UNLV had won 45 games in a row, including the National Championship game from the previous year when they beat us by 30 points, 103–73. Unlike the year before, this year's game was hard-fought, close, and incredibly exciting. Throughout the course of the game, usually only one basket separated the two teams' scores.

With under two and a half minutes remaining, UNLV jumped to a five-point lead and it seemed the momentum was going their way. When Bobby brought the ball down the court, I recognized that UNLV had changed from man-to-man defense to a

matchup zone. I jumped up off the bench to tell
Bobby to run a certain play against this new defense. Just as I got to my feet, Bobby took a three-
point shot and knocked it down. He did not need
my instruction, he needed to courageously follow
his instincts. As a result of that play, the momentum
shifted back and we were put in the position to win
the game in the last few seconds. Bobby's three-
pointer was as big a shot as any Duke player has
ever hit. After we beat UNLV, we won our first National Championship by beating Kansas 72–65.
Many people think of game-winning shots as last-
second shots. This is not always the case. Bobby's
courageous shot in the UNLV game is the perfect
example.

The following year, we again found ourselves in
the national semifinal game, this time matched up
against Indiana. The Hoosiers played an amazing
first half and really should have blown us right out
of the gym. However, Bobby hit four three-point
shots in that half to keep us within striking distance. We played well and together in the second
half and won, eventually beating Michigan for our
second straight National Championship. Neither
of those championships would be ours unless
Bobby had the courage to follow his instincts.

Courage is the capacity to confront what can be
imagined. We all have the capacity to imagine

amazing things, but you need courage to take those often frightening steps toward making your dreams a reality. Your time will come. As President John F. Kennedy once said, *"Courage is an opportunity that sooner or later is presented to all of us."*

Crisis
Management

As a leader, and particularly a leader in sport, I am often asked about how to act and lead your team in a time of crisis. My response is that, once you find yourself in that crisis moment, it may already be too late. If you have not developed your team properly, members of that team will not feel the sense of ownership your group needs in this type of moment.

Crises are not handled in the instant they occur but are prepared for in all of the moments that you and your team spend leading up to that one. You prepare for the crisis well ahead of time by establishing trusting relationships among all members of your team. For me, every team meeting, every practice, every individual conversation that occurs throughout the season establishes who we will collectively be when a crisis occurs. If you plan to manage a crisis when the time comes, it is already too late to establish the communication and trust that should already exist among the members of your team.

Crisis causes people to think and act as individuals rather than as part of a team. In difficult situations, it is human nature to feel alone, and you may start worrying about your personal plight as opposed to the unit as a whole. A leader's goal during these times must be to refocus every individual's attention on the group, the entity that you have created, which is far stronger than each separate individual. When you truly trust and rely on one another, you find strength in your unity and can face challenges with the courage and confidence that comes with knowing you are not in it alone.

In any profession, a crisis presents a situation in which it is the leader's job to find a way to win. Of course, my version of a crisis as a basketball coach is minimal when put into perspective. A crisis for me is being down by one point with only a few seconds on the clock, while others face terminal illness, being sent to war, and other life-or-death situations. No matter how strongly you feel about what you are doing, it is important that you keep a sense of perspective about the "crises" you face.

If you have a trusting team, business, or family, a crisis becomes an opportunity to shine. You relish the predicament because it is a chance to prove to yourselves and to show others the strength you have developed as a unit during the course of your time together. A well-prepared team embraces crises as defining moments and overcomes those crises together, as one.

CRISIS MANAGEMENT IN ACTION

One of the great basketball stories during my time at Duke was the 1992 NCAA regional championship game against the University of Kentucky. The winners would earn a trip to the Final Four and the losers would find themselves at their season's end. Many still refer to it as the greatest college basketball game ever played. Everyone who has seen the game recognizes the incredible passion and heart with which both our and the Kentucky kids played. It was truly a beautiful game.

The Kentucky game serves as a perfect illustration of team crisis management. With a trip to the Final Four on the line, I and my team found ourselves in overtime, down by one point with 2.1 seconds remaining on the clock. We had possession of the ball on one end of the court and had to score on the opposite basket, 94 feet away.

I had some great players and amazing young men on my team that year, including All-Americas Christian Laettner, Bobby Hurley, and Grant Hill.

As they came to the bench for that last timeout, I could see a look of defeat in their eyes. The first thing I said to them as they sat down in our huddle was, "We are going to win." Whether they believed this seemingly ridiculous claim or not, it had the effect of immediately focusing everyone's attention on our collective goal instead of thinking about blame, regret, fear, or what beach they would be going to next week instead of the Final Four.

Then I looked Grant Hill in the eye and asked him if he could pass the ball 75 feet to Christian Laettner, who would be waiting to receive the pass at the opposite free throw line. He responded that, yes, he could do that. I then turned to Christian, looked him in the eye, and asked him if he could catch the ball and get a shot off in the very short 2.1 seconds that remained in the game. He said to me, "Coach, if Grant throws a good pass, I'll catch it."

Both players said that they could and, more importantly, that they *would* accomplish their assigned tasks. They both made positive statements. I loved Hill's and Laettner's responses, because in their voices we heard confidence, and that confidence was felt throughout the entire team. It is so vital in a group for each member to hear the team message echoed by more than one voice. Christian and Grant both exuded confidence in themselves and in our team, and as a result, we left that huddle all feeling like we would be winners.

It all went according to plan. Grant threw the ball to Christian, as promised, and Christian caught the ball, dribbled once, turned around, and took our team's shot. The ball left his hand and, while it seemed to hang in the air forever, the clock expired. It went in. Pandemonium.

A lot of people say that we were lucky that day. I say, luck favors those who have spent their preparation time building effective systems of communication and trust in one another. That way, when a crisis occurs for you, within your family, your team, or your business, it can turn into an opportunity to shine.

Culture

*M*aking shots counts—but not as much as the people who make them.

Developing a culture means having a tradition that maintains the standards you want to define your program. A common mistake among those who work in sport is spending a disproportional amount of time on "x's and o's" as compared to time spent learning about people. Culture is established by the people who compose your team and is carried on through those people. In other words, culture can only exist through the relationships among the people who make up your group, those in the back offices and on the front lines. A successful development of culture means that you hear different voices echoing the same message throughout the organization—now, through the history of your program, and into its future. But you cannot merely expect culture to be a natural occurrence; it has to be taught and made a part of your everyday routine. Culture is a continuum. This means that it is not merely a matter of creating a culture, but perpetuating it. Those who have been in the organization for the greatest amount of time pass on the values and the message of the organization to those who are just entering. A recent trend in college basketball has seen many players leaving college early or forgoing their college career entirely to enter the NBA. While this has become virtually unavoidable, it does have a significant effect on the culture of individual programs and college basketball as a whole.

Recruiting is a key aspect of growing a culture. When my staff and I decide which kids to recruit, we don't merely look at the youngster's athletic ability, statistics, and grades, we look at how they treat their parents, how they interact with their classmates, and what other ways they contribute to their communities. One of my favorite things is when we go for a home visit and the player has his best friend with him, a friend who may not even play basketball. This shows that, at a young age, he understands that it's not all about him and he is willing to share his life with those close to him: an indication that he is willing to look beyond himself and become a part of something greater.

Culture is passing on the values and teaching

the standards that you have learned as an upper-classman to the young players on the team. I can re-member many practices during the 1986 season when my starting backcourt of Johnny Dawkins, a senior, and Tommy Amaker, a junior, would com-pletely dominate our second team.

Quin Snyder was a freshman on that second unit and would leave a number of practices feeling down and defeated. Johnny and Tommy would take Quin off to the side and tell him about when they had gone through those experiences as well. It was all a part of developing as an individual player and as a part of the Duke Basketball culture. They reminded Quin to keep working hard and keep listening to the coaching staff and that eventually it would all work out. Quin became a starter the next season and was one of our captains and major contributors on the 1989 Final Four team. He, in turn, spent time passing the lessons he learned on to Christian Laettner, who was a freshman on that 1989 team. Teaching culture is not just a leader's task; everyone on the team is responsible for passing the values, standards, and traditions on to the next generation. Christian passed it on to Grant Hill, Grant Hill to Jeff Capel, Jeff Capel to Trajan Langdon. And so on. And so on.

Dependability

Dependability is the ability to be relied upon. To always be there trying to do your best.

I have always admired Cal Ripken. Playing in a record 2,632 straight games, he earned a reputation as baseball's "Iron Man." What that means to me is that Cal played when he was sick, injured, tired: times when many other people would not have. It would be amazing to be Cal Ripken's teammate; you knew you could always depend on him. He was always there, giving his all. I try to encourage in my teams the importance of showing up and being at your best each and every day. Being able to depend on one another gives us the greatest chance of collectively achieving our goals.

Just like Cal Ripken was for the Baltimore Orioles, my brother, Bill Krzyzewski, is the Iron Man of our family. He retired recently as a captain in the

Chicago Fire Department, after thirty-seven years of service. In all of those thirty-seven years, my brother never missed one day of work. Whether it was a small fire or a terrible one, you could count on his being there and doing whatever was necessary to get the job done. Whenever I would go to the firehouse for a visit, some of Bill's men would take me aside and tell me how lucky I am that he is my brother. "He is always there for us," they would say. "We would follow him anywhere."

Bill is three and a half years older than I and we didn't really "run in the same circles" growing up. Our interests and talents were different and so were our friends, but we were always brothers. I could always count on that. If there was a problem, Bill would take care of it. He would handle it in the best possible fashion and he would never, ever say, "You owe me." He didn't do it because he wanted anything in return, he did it because he was my older brother and he loved me, and that is what older brothers are supposed to do. We all need heroes. My brother is my hero.

Dependability is not only about being there physically, but being there at your best. It is about loyalty and commitment, about being someone on whom your teammates can count. You don't have to have a master's degree to teach dependability; you teach it by example. I learned it from Bill.

I have often told my brother, "I could never be as good a brother to you as you have been to me. You are the guy I have counted on and looked up to for my whole life."

My greatest honor is when my hero, my Iron Man, looks back at me and tells me, "I love who you've become." Knowing that my brother was always there for me has helped me immensely. I tell Bill, "I love who *we* have become." All this would not have happened unless Bill was there.

Empathy

Empathy: the ability to walk in another person's shoes.

As a coach, a parent, or a leader of any kind, one of the most important things that you can feel for one of your "teammates" is empathy. If someone believes that you can identify with their situation and understand their feelings, they are more apt to trust you, which leads to faster responses to situations and better conclusions.

Empathy is important not only in coaching man-to-man defense, but in helping to soothe a daughter with a broken heart. In either situation, though the feelings involved are completely different, empathy means having the ability to, most literally, feel what the other person is feeling. Then they will never feel alone.

Showing empathy for someone can help them

to develop empathy for others. My oldest daughter, Debbie, who is now an incredible mother to her four children, told me an amazing thing. She told me that I taught her how to empathize. And I remember just the moment she was talking about. She had come home from Duke after a rough breakup with a longtime boyfriend and was completely heartbroken. She cried and talked to my wife, Mickie, for hours. Finally, emotionally exhausted, she fell asleep lying across her bed. She said that the first thing she remembers after that is waking up with me sitting on the bed next to her and gently patting her back. When she turned to look at me, I was crying too. "Dad, what's wrong?" she asked. I replied, "I just feel so sad for you." It was true. Her heartbreak was my heartbreak too; that's what makes us a family and the greatest of teams. For a person to know that someone else understands their feelings really validates those feelings. Once acknowledged or validated, the person has a greater chance of moving on to something better, instead of being a prisoner of that particular feeling.

Part of being on any team, and a family team in particular, is trying to truly understand what each of your teammates is going through. If you feel true empathy, it can be a beautiful thing. Their difficult times become your difficult times and, likewise, their successes become your successes. Either way, your collective moments become better, less sad, or more celebratory. Someone else feels what you feel. It is not about each of us individually but, rather, all of us together. Empathy brings your group closer together by allowing all members of the group to feel as if all of their feelings are truly a shared experience.

Enthusiasm

Enthusiasm is a great interest or excitement. When you are enthusiastic, you are a catalyst to those around you. Your unabashed love and emotion for what you are doing is contagious.

As a coach, many people may think that my job is about giving: giving instruction, giving advice, giving encouragement. But when I look into the eyes of someone like Chris Collins, it is hard to explain how much I receive in return. Chris was the captain of the 1996 team and is now one of my assistant coaches. When he was a player, I saw the enthusiasm written across his face, and it fueled me. I was lucky to coach him and now am fortunate to have him on my staff, where he can share his enthusiasm for the game of basketball with our current players.

Chris Collins was the embodiment of enthusiasm. He loved to get the crowd into the game; he loved to slap the floor; he loved to get excited. Quite simply, he loved to play basketball. But my favorite part about Chris's enthusiasm is that it was not singular. It was plural. He would be even more excited about a great play made by a teammate than one he made himself.

Chris was a part of our Duke teams during a very difficult stretch, one in which we went from having a 28–6 season in 1994 to being 13–18 the following year. This was the year in which I was forced to take off the majority of the season due to my health, and it created a time of great concern for the future of the program. Let's just say it was a difficult time to be enthusiastic.

When I returned to coaching in 1996, Chris's senior year, we had a great group of young men, but the talent level was not as high as other Duke teams I've coached. In January, we headed to North Carolina State for a conference road game. We had lost four games in a row and our record in the Atlantic Coast Conference was 0–4. Since we had placed last in the ACC the previous year, many feared we were headed in that same direction. In many ways, it felt as if the direction of not just our season but our program hung in the balance of that game. We could win and be rejuvenated or lose and have our morale further decreased.

In a hard-fought battle, Chris's unwavering enthusiasm served as the emotional backbone for the rest of our team. N.C. State was ahead 68–63 with 1:30 to go in the game. Jeff Capel drove to the basket and had his shot blocked and the ball began to go out of bounds near half-court. Chris chased down the ball and dove over the scorer's table to send it back inbounds to Ricky Price. But Chris did not stop there. He immediately got up and ran back onto the court, receiving a pass from Ricky and hitting a three-point shot to cut State's lead to two. With the short amount of time left on the clock, we made the strategic decision to foul and send N.C. State to the free throw line. After they hit both of their free throws, Jeff Capel drove and quickly scored on the offensive end, putting us within two points once again. With 16 seconds left, we fouled again, and this time the State player missed the front end of a one-and-one free throw opportunity.

On our last possession of the game, Chris dribbled up the court to where we had drawn up a play for him to hand the ball off to Ricky Price. However, instead of handing the ball off, Chris's instincts told him to shoot. With six seconds left on the clock, he fired up a three-pointer and, after spending what felt like forever bouncing on the rim, the ball fell through the net. We won 71–70.

Chris remained our leader for the rest of the season, in which we finished 18–13 overall and 8–8 in conference play. The N.C. State game had been a springboard for Chris and the rest of our team. During the last month of the season, Chris was not only our emotional leader, he was our best player, averaging close to 27 points a game. His contagious enthusiasm led us to the NCAA tournament in a year we were not expected to make it. The following year, and in fact the next five seasons in a row, we won the conference regular season championship.

Chris Collins's undying enthusiasm set the program back on the right path. Despite the difficult times, Chris never allowed his spirit to be defeated, and as a result he was the catalyst for getting the Duke program back on the path to success. Being excited about playing and being a part of a team is easy to do when you are winning 30 games a year and contending for championships. But it becomes more difficult when you are losing, when fans and the media are taking shots at you, and when it feels as if nothing is working. Chris's enthusiasm was particularly impressive because he showed it at a very high level even when it was difficult to do so.

I often refer to Chris as "the bridge." He is the guy that led us over a difficult season and connected the success of the 1994 Final Four team with the future success of Duke Basketball. In 2000, Chris returned to Duke as an assistant coach. That 2000–01 season, we won our third National Championship. I was so happy to share that with Chris Collins, who deserved it as much as any kid I have ever coached.

Of his time at Duke, Chris has said, "If there's one thing that I would like to be remembered for when I leave Duke, it's that that kid just really loved to play the game." And Duke fans *will* never forget the enthusiasm of Chris Collins.

Excellence

When I sign autographs for kids, I almost always put the same message: "Always try your best." If they get nothing else from meeting me, I want them to remember these words.

Excellence is not measured the same way for everyone. A .500 season may be a perfect standard of success for one team, while a National Championship is the standard for another. Define your own success and failure; only *you* know whether or not you have given it your all. The persistent pursuit of excellence determines winners, not the score of the game.

To be excellent, you must be yourself. Do the very best that you can do. In giving your best every day, improvement will come naturally. Giving your all makes you better; it's that simple. Remember that there is a vital distinction between excellence and perfection. If you ask a young person to be excellent, he or she may think, "Oh, man, I have to be perfect? I can't do that." But if you ask him or her to just give their personal best, anybody can do that.

In the context of a team, there are many times when you are not the best individual on the team in a particular activity. You can sometimes have the tendency to look at the best person and say that he or she is excellent and you are not. This is a big mistake. Each person can be excellent, but one person may have more ability or expertise at a given time and in a given situation. This happens every year on a basketball team. What I tell my players is, "You have to *run your own race* individually while we are running our collective race as a team."

In 1998, Elton Brand and Shane Battier were both freshmen and starters for us at Duke. Elton became one of the best players in the country his first year and was National Player of the Year the next. Shane was not at that level of play immediately, but still played excellent basketball. He was a starter and was named National Defensive Player of the Year as a sophomore. Shane averaged only about 9 points a game that season, far fewer than Elton's 17. However, he always had a high opinion of his accomplishments and he was never jealous. He never felt frustrated about his efforts because he did not compare them to Elton's. Elton left Duke before his junior year and was the number one pick in the NBA draft. Shane stayed and became an all-conference player, and in his senior year was the National Player of the Year, just like Elton had been. They both ran different races, and achieved equal excellence.

Another part of seeking and maintaining excellence is always surrounding yourself with others who have high personal standards. Sometimes, when you are not at your best, someone else will be, and they can help raise you to that level.

I learned about excellence from my college coach, Bob Knight. I was the point guard for Coach Knight at West Point for three years. During that time, I learned what it meant to pursue excellence. Coach demanded that from us every day and it was a great lesson for me to learn. Coach Knight is one of the best leaders I have ever known.

After I graduated from West Point and finished my five-year service commitment to the United States Army, I was presented with the opportunity to join Coach Knight's Indiana University staff as a graduate assistant. This was another great chance for me to be around him and his team. During this experience, I met some other excellent coaches, most notably Hall of Fame coaches Henry Iba and Pete Newell. Both of these legendary coaches told me that I had an incredible opportunity to learn from the best in Coach Knight. And they gave me some advice that I will never forget. They told me to learn absolutely everything I could from Coach, to soak up his theories and philosophies, his genius for the game, and his ability to motivate. But they also told me not to try to *be* Coach Knight or anyone else, but to take everything that I learned from him and fit it into who I am as a person, a leader, and a coach. Essentially, they told me to be myself.

It is overwhelming to tell someone that they have to be Michael Jordan or Grant Hill or Ernest Hemingway or Albert Einstein. They will think it impossible. Our goal should not be to *be* our heroes, but rather to *learn* from them and then do the best possible job of being ourselves. That is how I define excellence.

Failure

Winning does not define who I am. Don't get me wrong—I am competitive and I love to win, but it does not define me.

Growing up, I knew what I was good at and I stuck to it. As a result, I became captain of my high school basketball team, a member of the national honor society, and vice president of my class. But going to school, playing basketball, and leading—these were all things that came naturally to me. I played it safe and I didn't venture beyond what was comfortable and easy for me.

My first real experience with failure came when I went to West Point. There, failure was a common occurrence for me. I didn't know how to tie a knot, I didn't know how to swim, and, growing up in inner-city Chicago, I had never had much experience with the great outdoors. At West Point, you were expected either to already know these things or learn them *very* quickly.

I learned so much at West Point both as an individual and as a member of a team. A major part of this learning process was stepping out of the realm of what came naturally, attempting new things, and, sometimes, failing at those things. I learned from West Point, and have tried to pass the message along to my teams, that progress is impossible if you only attempt to do the things that you have always done.

As an individual at West Point, I experienced my first failure when I did not pass my fall semester physical education requirement. For an all-state basketball player and someone who was considered a better than average athlete, this was the ultimate failure. The two PE courses I had that semester were swimming and gymnastics. I knew from the beginning that this would be problematic. I did not know how to swim and I had never tried gymnastics, nor any athletic endeavor that required flexibility. Everything was completely foreign to me. Though I was able to pass gymnastics by a very slim margin, I failed the swimming class and had to join a remedial swimming course until I passed the survival swimming test. The test consisted of being handed a ten-pound brick and being told to swim as far as I could, with the brick, in a seven-foot-deep pool. After I pushed away from the side, the brick went to the bottom of the pool and so did I. It was not surprising that my grade sunk as well.

The inability to pass this test the first time around and the resulting failing grade in physical education forced me to take a test with a number of other cadets to prove that I was physically capable of staying at the Academy. That test did not include swimming or gymnastics and I was able to pass with flying colors. Failing initially, but working hard to learn enough about swimming to pass the swimming test as well led me to understand that I could eventually do things that I had never done before.

My failures at the Academy were not limited to individual endeavors; I met with group failure as well. As freshmen, our platoon was asked at times to change from one uniform to another in a very short period of time. We would be told to dismiss from a formation, go back to our rooms, change to a different uniform, and be back in the same formation within three minutes. To me, this was impossible. The first time around, everyone panicked and tried to accomplish this feat completely on their own. I remember my two roommates and I ran into each other, pushed one another, and all of us were late in coming back out to formation. The upperclassman in charge of the formation asked us why we were late. The only permissible answer was, "No excuse, sir."

"That's right. There is no excuse," he said. "All of you should be out here on time." The next time we were put in this situation, one of my roommates miraculously made it out in time, but my other roommate and I were late. The upperclassman then yelled at all three of us, saying, "Either all of you are going to be late or you will all be on time." After many such situations, we made the realization that we would need to employ teamwork to be ready in time. When we worked together to be ready, we finally all made it on time to the formation. In that situation, failure forced us to find a way to help one another succeed.

Changing limits is not easy. If it was, everyone would do it without a second thought. One of the biggest lessons I have learned in my life is that failure is a natural result of breaking out of your comfort zone. At West Point, I learned to view each failure not as its own entity but as a stepping-stone on a path to something greater. It was never a destination, but I had to pass through failure to be successful at what I was attempting to do. In order to change what you believe to be your limits, you have to try new things or raise your old limits to a new level.

I had to recall this lesson throughout my life

and career because, like most people, I have failed time and time again. I can remember my third season at Duke. The group of freshmen I had that year was one of my top recruiting classes in all my years of coaching: Mark Alarie, Jay Bilas, Johnny Dawkins, David Henderson, and Weldon Williams. We had an incredible amount of talent that year but not much experience. When we ended the season with 11 wins and 17 losses, I had to teach my team that what happened was part of a process. We used that season as a learning experience and were able to look to the future: a future that we all expected would be bright. As Johnny Dawkins put it twenty years later, "We knew we were better than that, but that is where our journey began."

And because we saw that 1982–83 season as a stepping-stone on the way to something greater, the rest of our journey was incredible. The next three seasons, we had an 84–21 record, and in 1986 we won 37 games, which is still the most ever won by a college basketball team in a single season.

No one can be perfect. When you break out of your comfort zone and try new things, you will probably experience some form of failure. Failure cannot be your final destination; rather, you can use it to shatter limits. It is merely a stepping-stone on your journey to greatness.

Family

No matter how involved you are in what you do, no matter how many hours a week you devote to your career pursuits, you must always remember that your family is your primary team.

Most likely due to the fact that I have been a basketball coach for so many years, my family has always thought of itself as parallel to a basketball team. Our nucleus includes five people: myself, my wife, and our three daughters, like the five players on the basketball court at any given time. While each of us has a life and interests that are our own, we gather strength from that nucleus. We're in this together.

Over the years, each of our daughters has married and we have been blessed with five grandchildren, who call me "Poppy." We have never seen it as our children leaving, but rather as expanding our strong core. There come times in our lives when any one of us may need to "circle the wagons." In other words, when key decisions need to be made, when there is a crisis, when one of us is sick or needs help, we bring our core group together, we try to ignore other influences, and we rely on one another as teammates to develop a collective resolution.

A huge part of ensuring that your core is strong is allowing the members of your team to be a part of what you do. I always wanted my wife, my girls, and now my sons-in-law and grandchildren to be a part of what I am doing at Duke. They are not merely invited to practices, games, and team trips; I encourage them to be there if they can. I tell them about things I am trying with my team, ask for their advice on any problems, and watch game tapes with them. My girls grew up watching game film and tapes with me in our home, whether it was to analyze our team's practices and games to see how we could improve, or to scout our upcoming opponents' strengths and weaknesses. I remember when my girls were young, they would love when a reel of film would be over and there would be a white light shining from the projector onto the wall. For the next few minutes, we would do shadow puppets together. I'm not sure that they liked analyzing the film at that age, but I know they liked the shadow puppets. They were a welcome break for me as well.

Because my family has always felt like a part of Duke Basketball too, it was easier when I had to be away for long periods of time on road trips and recruiting. I never compartmentalized my career and my family. They are both a part of who I am, and being good in one can help tremendously with the other.

Additionally, when you allow those closest to you to be involved, they will be better able to support you in your times of need. And you have to let them. I remember a specific moment of family support following a tough season-ending loss to Kansas in the 2003 NCAA tournament. After the game, my family joined me in the locker room area, including my two young grandsons, Joey and Michael, who were three and a half and two years old, respectively. As we stood there in the coach's locker room, with several adults around me, Joey came confidently up to me, tugged gently on my pants leg, looked me in the eye, and said, "Don't be sad, Poppy. Your boys played really hard." It brought a smile to my face and set me at ease, and, what's more, he was right. My boys had played really hard. That's the kind of support you can get from your family, even a three-year-old member of that family, if you can allow them to be a part of your entire life.

While allowing my daughters to be a part of my career, my wife was always adamant that there be things devoted strictly to family. In fact, when the girls were growing up, there was nothing related to Duke Basketball put on display in our home: no trophies, photos, or memorabilia. We always believed that a home is about family, so we surrounded our home with family photos and items reflecting the accomplishments of our children. Your children must always believe that what they are doing and what you do as a family is the top priority.

A person is never more comfortable than when they are with their family, which is why I try to create a family atmosphere with my team and encourage people in other businesses to do the same with their employees and organization. When you are with your family, you are yourself, and when you are yourself, you are at your very best.

FAMILY IN ACTION

In 1994, we were in Charlotte, North Carolina, where Duke was playing in the Final Four. We were set to play the University of Florida in the Saturday night game in order to advance to the National Championship game. My middle daughter, Lindy, was still in high school and was going to finish out the school week before joining us for the games that weekend. One afternoon after school, she had gone to a local shopping center to run some errands. As she was getting out of her car, she was carjacked by a man with a gun. Luckily, Lindy was not injured and was able to get away and run to a police substation in the mall. Needless to say, it was a frightening incident, especially for a seventeen-year-old kid whose parents were out of town!

We asked Assistant Coach Tommy Amaker's wife, Stephanie, a successful area psychologist, and a part of our extended Duke Basketball family, to bring Lindy to Charlotte right away. After hugging her and telling her how happy we were that she was safe, my wife and I sat down with her and began to ask her a barrage of questions. How are you feeling? What did he say to you? Did you see the weapon? How did you get away? Did you see his face?

After answering a lot of questions, Lindy became exhausted, and, in reality, she was also beginning to move on from that moment and feel excited to be at the Final Four. Even so, my wife asked her, "What was he wearing?"

"A black shirt, jeans, and a baseball cap."

"Was there anything on the cap?" I asked.

With a look of exasperation and an obvious desire to move past the topic, Lindy looked me in the eye and said, "Yeah . . . Florida!"

While his hat, obviously, did not really say Florida, this was Lindy's way of telling me that she appreciated our concern but, enough about her, it was time for me to focus on why we were there: on beating Florida. What an amazing gesture of support from my daughter. While still concerned for her well-being, I could focus on the task at hand, knowing that I had her full support. We beat Florida and had the opportunity to play in the National Championship game. That kind of support is what family is all about.

Friendship

There is nothing more valuable than a true friend. They remind you of who you were, who you are now, and who you are going to be. They keep you both grounded and going in the right direction. Sometimes listening to a friend is like listening to yourself. They can be your conscience and your memory.

My very best friend is named Dennis Mlynski, but I have always called him "Moe" since we were boys growing up in Chicago. And to him and my other boyhood buddies, I will always be "Mick." He has been one of my greatest supporters throughout my life and career. Moe is the gold standard of friends. He is a better friend to me than I am to anyone, and I consider myself a good friend.

Every success that I have ever felt, Moe has felt

it too. Every failure I have experienced, he has put into perspective for me. He has been there every step of my journey, and I have been there for his. We have never been alone because we always know we have each other.

Specifically, this past year, after our season-ending loss to Louisiana State University in the Sweet Sixteen, Moe came to my hotel room along with my family. Long after everyone else had gone to bed, Moe, my wife, Mickie, and I were still talking. At the end of every season, I struggle with what I could have done differently, how I could have done better, and I reevaluate where I am in my life and career.

Feeling as down as I could be, I found myself wondering if coaching was still what I wanted to be doing, contemplating what was next for me. "Mick," Moe said to me, and even just hearing the name from my youth brought me back to earth. "You have always loved to lead." He put it so simply that I couldn't help but realize that he was right. I started that evening feeling down and wondering if I wanted to continue coaching. Thanks to Moe and his friendship, we ended our conversation at 5:30 in the morning with my being incredibly excited about the next season. That is what a friend does. He or she will listen to your ramblings, and because they know you so well and you can trust them to be honest and genuine, they help you clarify those ramblings.

As you grow and change, your true friends become friends to your family as well. I learned from my son-in-law about how Moe's friendship transcends generations. Chris Spatola, who is married to my youngest daughter, was an Army captain on a yearlong tour in Baghdad, Iraq. He told me that he had received several packages from Moe, including some long and wonderful letters. Chris, like me, had played basketball for the United States Military Academy at West Point. Moe also included in his packages to Chris several game programs and newspaper clippings about me and my teams from when I played at West Point. I couldn't believe it. Not only had Moe been there for so many of those games, not only had he saved those programs and clippings for more than thirty-five years, but he thought enough about me and my family to know that Chris would appreciate those things. My family feels lucky that Moe has become a part of their lives too.

True friends are with you for life, they remind you of the things that you need to know at the points in your life when you need to know them most. They care for you and try to clarify things for you during difficult times. And, most amazingly, friends like Moe never ask for anything in return. In life, there are not many absolutes, but when you have a great friend, that is an absolute. And Moe is *absolutely* the best friend in the world.

Fundamentals

When you have been in a particular business for a long time or, for me, when you have been through a long season of basketball, you can find yourself getting caught up in the complexities of what you are doing and forget about the fundamentals. It is important to remind yourself and your team of the essential building blocks of the game and to ensure that you continue to practice and improve on these. These building blocks are like the soil from which your skills grow. Practice will help keep that soil fertile.

At a dinner in the beautiful Wynn Las Vegas resort, I was reminded of the importance of fundamentals by a most unexpected source. My friend Steve Wynn, who, along with his wife, Elaine, has built some of the most phenomenal resorts in the

world, told me the profoundly simple concept behind their most recent masterpiece.

He told me that when approaching the building of his new hotel and casino, the first to bear the
Wynn name, he just went back to the basics. After
building such amazing places such as the Mirage
and Bellagio, it had become clear to him that there
was little "new" he could do in the hotel business.

Instead, Steve returned to the fundamentals.
The guiding thought behind the building of the
Wynn resort was, as Steve put it, "*doing the basics, better.*" Steve and Elaine spent the next several years
doing a multitude of basics better, such as ensuring
that the sheets were of the best quality, that each
room be a manageable distance from the elevators,
and that each area of the hotel had a pleasant and
welcoming scent. And, having been a guest at the
Wynn, I can assure you that the basics there are absolutely the best.

It is the same in basketball, or in any business.
I sometimes find myself devising complicated
schemes, trying to be more creative. Because I have
been coaching for so many years, I sometimes forget that a team, even a veteran team, needs a solid
foundation. Steve Wynn is right, I need to remind
myself that you can be the best in the business by
merely doing the basics, better.

To help turn fundamentals into habit requires

intensive, intelligent, and repetitive action. If any one of these elements is missing, something will be missing from the foundation of your team. This is why, in every practice, even late in the season, I always have my team continue to work on fundamental drills. It is vital that the athletes actually drill these basics. I constantly remind myself of the most basic formula of teaching: you hear, you forget; you see, you remember; you do, you understand. And when you truly understand, that is when the basics become habitual.

Every summer, we host a basketball camp at Duke for youngsters ages eight to eighteen who come from all over the world to learn from me and my staff how we do the fundamentals. One of the campers' mothers came up to me at registration and told me that her son would be attending two of the three sessions. I thought to myself, "This is great, she really understands the importance of learning how to drill the fundamentals." But then she asked me what her son would be doing differently in his second week of camp. I explained to her that the second week would be more of the same. There would be different coaches and different competition, but the focus would continue to be on the basics of basketball. I explained to her about fundamentals becoming habits and how the drills we do in camp are a step toward that. What's more,

I told her that her son would be in even better shape if he continued to work on the drills when he returned home after his two weeks at camp. If you want to strive for excellence, you must embrace continual work on fundamentals.

I think it's amazing that everyone—from a young kid going to summer camp to someone as successful as Steve Wynn—can always remember that *with intensive, intelligent, and repetitive work, we can all do the basics, better.*

Giving Back

Ｉt is not all about winning games. There are much greater battles to fight. As I have grown older and experienced some success, I have learned that when you use your success to have a positive impact in these other battles, it adds depth to your life. Having a positive influence on people, helping others: that's winning.

For someone to be a total human being, they must realize that something happened before them, something is happening now, and something will happen after they leave. As I have become involved with more community service, I have felt more complete. The feeling of winning a basketball game, or even a National Championship, is much deeper when it leads to the feeling that comes with raising money for the Duke Children's Hospital, building the Emily Krzyzewski Family Life Center, and the feeling that will come when doctors and scientists discover a cure for cancer.

Many people give money to charities. This is a great thing to do, as many of these organizations and foundations need these funds in order to pursue their mission. However, not everyone has the ability to give financially. One thing we can all give is *time*. And this is absolutely the most valuable thing you can give to another person, a group, or a charitable organization. When you spend time with someone in need or contribute to a cause, you really become a part of that person or a part of that endeavor. The feeling you have is addictive. It is a unique feeling knowing that you have gotten outside of yourself and made a positive impact on someone else.

I always remind myself that I came from somewhere. Where did I start? I was not a Hall of Fame coach or a public figure my whole life. Who helped me? I know I did not get here alone. There were people who helped me along the way. Everyone needs people like that. This is why I am a strong advocate of mentorship programs. Such programs give children a chance to be around and learn from positive influences. Often the impact you have on these youngsters will lead them to have a similar impact on someone else. Giving back breeds giving back. It is simply the right thing to do.

I also try to keep in perspective how lucky my family and I have been to have our health. Some people are not so lucky and they need others to help boost their morale and help them heal mentally and emotionally, as well as great doctors to help them get well physically. Cancer has had an impact on nearly everyone. In my life, it took my mom and my friend Jim Valvano. As a member of the board of the Jimmy V Foundation for Cancer Research, I believe that, through the hard work of the doctors and scientists who research the disease, as well as other foundations like the Jimmy V, we will eventually win this battle. I have always been amazed at how many courageous people I have met through these endeavors. These friendships are cherished by me and my family.

Sometimes in life you need people to remind you of the necessity to move outside yourself and give back to the people and community around you. P.J. Carlesimo, one of my friends and an assistant coach for the San Antonio Spurs, often serves as that reminder for me. He will call me up and say, "Hey, One-Way." This is his way of reminding me not to be a "one-way" type of guy. In life, I have been given a lot, but it is not a one-way street. I must remember to give back, to be a two-way person. Utilizing the success I have achieved to have a positive impact on people is what makes my life fulfilling. Usually whatever I have given, I get back more.

No matter who you are or what you have achieved, you are incomplete until you find a way to use the blessings you have experienced in your life to have a positive effect on others. For me, it is not all about winning games but, rather, how we can use the success that we achieve on the court to contribute to the greater good.

Guidance

Guidance is help. We all need it. How do we get it? And how do we give it?

When someone you care about asks for guidance, it is often difficult to know exactly what to say. After all, it is their life, not yours, and they know more about the entirety of the situation than you do. But because you care for them, often you will try to put yourself in their shoes and to help in any way you can. As a leader and, more importantly, as a teacher, it is crucial to know how to properly offer guidance. It is something that is very difficult to do and something at which very few people are good.

Father Rog, a geometry teacher at my high school, Weber, knew exactly how to give guidance. I grew up in a very strict Catholic family and attended Catholic boys' school all my life. My faith was important to me but there were many things

about it that I did not completely understand.
When I was a teenager, I had many questions, but,
because of my upbringing, these were difficult to
ask. At times, I really did not know how to put them
into words. And at other times, I just didn't want to
ask because I might appear foolish. Fear of looking
foolish is a common impediment in the lives of
teenagers.

Because Father Rog had been my teacher and
had worked a lot with the athletes at Weber, I had
grown to trust him. He knew me well enough to
see when I was troubled by something. One day, he
asked me to sit down with him in an empty cafete-
ria after one of our basketball practices. He said, "I
know you have some things on your mind. Why
don't you tell me about them." Then he did the
best thing you can possibly do for a troubled
youngster: *he listened.* He did it intently and he did
not interrupt. Then he tried to help me clarify
what I was really asking. And finally, in offering his
counsel, he didn't simply provide me with an answer. Rather, he led me down a path where the
solution would be mine to discover. I finally got answers to questions that I either did not know how
or was too afraid to ask.

I have continued to seek Father Rog's counsel
and wisdom throughout my life. And each time, he
has reminded me about what it means to offer

guidance. You do just that: you *guide*. You can go to someone you trust and respect to point out a path, but remember: *solutions are personal.* They are yours. You must take ownership of them.

As a college basketball coach, I work with young men who are experiencing a great deal of change in their lives. The transition from high school to college is a giant mental and emotional leap. I am a part of their lives during this impressionable time. And, again, I am their coach, friend, and advocate as they make the equally great transition from college to the real world.

During these tenuous times, I recognize that these young men are likely experiencing the same sort of feelings and questions that I had when I first sought the counsel of Father Rog. I know that I cannot merely give them the answer that worked for me back then, or even answers that have worked for my other players in the past. Just because the resolution I came to worked for me does not mean it will work for them. My job is to point them to a path where they can discover their own solution. Then the solution is *theirs* and they are more apt to stick by it and even be proud of it. In offering a path as opposed to an answer, you put people in the position to follow that path again and again when new and different problems arise throughout their lives.

Imagination

Everybody has the ability to imagine. However, this gift is often underutilized by today's youth. In a world of video games and mp3 players, too often youngsters are entertained by someone imagining for them.

I can remember playing basketball, all alone, in a Chicago schoolyard as a kid. I would take jump shots, drive to the hoop for layups, shoot free throws, all the while verbalizing a running commentary of the game that I was playing in my head. "Down by one . . . 79–78 . . . six seconds on the clock . . . Krzyzewski dribbling down the court, crosses over . . . 3 . . . 2 . . . 1 . . ."

As I took that final shot, I felt like I was really there, that the game was really on the line, and that I had the chance to be a hero. If the shot went in, the final buzzer sounded and I celebrated the victory. If I missed, there was, of course, a foul on the play and the game continued as I stood at the free throw line with no time on the clock. Though I enacted a broad range of imaginary scenarios throughout my youth, one thing remained the same: when I imagined, I always won!

Imagination gives you a destination. When you dream, and you feel what it is like to be inside that dream, you feel inspired to make that dream a reality. You begin a process, a journey, toward making real those feelings that you first found in your imagination.

In my career as a basketball coach, I have been in countless end-of-game pressure situations that can bring about nerves and anxiety. But because I imagined myself in these positions as a kid, I have always felt like I've been there before. The mind is so powerful. If you commit to utilizing your imagination to envision positive things, you will come to truly believe those things.

In early 2006, we opened a community center in downtown Durham, North Carolina, for children from low socioeconomic backgrounds. I am so proud that the center was named in honor of my late mother, whose hard work and commitment to family provided me and my brother with opportunities to imagine. The Emily Krzyzewski Family Life Center's motto is "Dream, Do, Achieve." In other words, the center and its programs strive to inspire youngsters to dream of a better future, provide them with opportunities to develop their fundamental skills, and, ultimately, promote achievement through the development of character, capability, and confidence. The foundation of this pathway toward achievement is in dreams, in imagination.

The greatest gift a coach can give a player, a teacher can give a student, and a parent can give to their child is the opportunity to imagine great things. These dreams in childhood pave the way for future successes.

IMAGINATION IN ACTION

Following the 1999 season in which we lost to the University of Connecticut in the National Championship game, several of our players decided to leave school early, either entering the NBA draft or transferring to another school. Shane Battier was one of the players who would return for two more seasons. Though he was a key player and starter on the team, Shane had averaged only about eight points a game and contributed to the team more as a role player than a star.

My staff and I knew that in order for us to be successful in the coming seasons, Shane was going to need to maximize his potential and become our star. The only problem was that he had never thought of himself as a star; he had never imagined it. He was much too humble. I told Shane after that 1999 season that he was going to have to spend the off-season imagining himself in a starring role.

That summer, as a follow-up to that conversation, I called Shane and asked him, "Shane, this morning while you were shaving, did you look in the mirror and imagine that you were looking at next year's conference player of the year?"

He chuckled and began to respond, "Coach, c'mon, I didn't . . ."

Click. I hung up the phone.

The next day, I called him again and this time asked, "When you were on your way to your internship this morning, did you picture yourself going for 30 points against Virginia?"

Again, Shane responded with a cautious laugh.

I hung up on him again.

A few seconds later, my phone rang and it was Shane. "Coach, don't hang up on me!"

"I won't hang up on you if *you* won't hang up on you. We made a deal that you would imagine those things." Shane needed to imagine because, by doing so, when the time came and he actually found himself in those situations, he would feel as if he had already been there.

That next season, Shane averaged nearly 18 points and six rebounds a game and was first team

All–Atlantic Coast Conference. A year later, in his senior season, he earned National Player of the Year and National Defensive Player of the Year honors and led our team to the 2001 National Championship.

He always possessed the tools necessary to be a star and a great leader, and he was always incredibly talented and smart, but Shane only fully realized his potential when he allowed himself to imagine great things. As a result, his teammates and I were able to go along for the ride as all of Shane Battier's dreams came true.

Integrity

Integrity means doing what is right whether you are alone or with a group, doing the right thing no matter what the rewards or the consequences may be. It means putting your base of ethics into action.

It takes strength of character to have integrity. Imagine yourself in a group of four kids. One is urging the rest of you to do something that you know is not right. Peer pressure is a powerful thing and can cause people to do things that are completely against their personal code. By saying no and not allowing yourself to fall victim to the pressure, you may be providing the other two individuals with the strength they need to say no as well. Perhaps they, too, knew it was wrong but simply were not strong enough to take a stand. You can walk away from the situation feeling proud that you stood your ground and that maybe you helped someone else find the strength to do so as well.

I learned about integrity in the simplest possible way; my parents told me to do the right thing. So it was no surprise for me when I wound up at West Point, which operates under a strict code of ethics. The honor code states, "A cadet will not lie, cheat, steal, or tolerate those who do." If you have integrity, and you can count on the others around you, your teammates, to be ethical as well, imagine the strength that you can form as a team: an entire group of individuals committed to simply doing the right thing.

I have always told my teams and my three daughters that getting a D on a test, or even in a course, is far from the worst thing one can do. You can recover from that. You can study harder for the next test, you can get a tutor, you can even retake the course. The only bad thing would be if you were to cheat. *Cheating means you are giving up on yourself.* You lose a piece of yourself each time you violate your personal sense of what is right and what is wrong.

Giving up on your integrity is a dangerous thing. One slip can lead to another, and before you know it, you may forget your ethics completely. With each violation, it becomes easier, and you feel less and less like what you are doing is wrong. However, if you stand by your code of ethics no matter what, your foundation becomes stronger and it becomes increasingly easy to follow your code through even the most trying times.

INTEGRITY IN ACTION

When I was a kid, I remember my father used to carry a lot of change in his pants pocket; you could hear it as he walked down the hall. Each day when he came home from work, he would hang his work pants over the back of a chair in his bedroom. One afternoon, knowing that he was in another room, I sneaked into their bedroom and took a small amount of change from his pants pocket. Surely there was so much of it that he would never notice. I took the coins, bought some candy that I had wanted, and enjoyed it.

The next day, my father called me into his room and asked me if I had taken the change from his pocket. I was scared that I would certainly be in trouble, so I lied and told him that I had not. As it turns out, one of the coins I had taken happened to have some sentimental value to my father; it was his lucky coin. It seemed pretty unlucky to me.

Now I realize how lucky that coin really was. My dad told me that he was very disappointed. Not only did I steal, but also I followed that up with a lie. One unethical thing led to another.

I remember how I felt that afternoon. I had disappointed my dad, but, even worse, I had let myself down. I am glad I got caught that day. It set me on a path where I knew I never wanted to feel that way again. From that point on, I have tried to live my whole life with integrity. Doing the right thing becomes easier with time and repetition. Eventually, your integrity becomes an integral part of who you are and your ethics serve as a moral guide in all of life's decisions.

Learning

To me, living *is* learning. Once you stop learning, you are no longer living.

Even as someone who considers himself a teacher, one of the most important things I always try to recognize is that I never stop learning. Of course, I have learned an incredible amount from my parents, my wife, and my teachers and coaches throughout my life. But you do not merely learn from these traditional teaching sources. As a teacher, you can learn from your students. As a CEO, from your employees. As a parent, from your children. The key to learning is *listening*. I try to make it a habit to listen to everyone.

Tommy Amaker is the first great point guard that I ever had at Duke. He had tremendous poise. He came to Duke already prepared to play at the ACC level as a freshman. He had incredible instincts about the game, particularly on the defensive end. In his first two practices as a freshman, I remember teaching a defensive stance, specifically used when putting pressure on the opponent with the ball. I was in my ninth year as a head coach and I had been taught that the proper way to guard the ball was with your palms up. Tommy was playing pressure defense and he had his palms down, but he was doing a great job!

Regardless, I stopped the drill and told Tommy that he needed to have his palms up when guarding the ball. When Tommy asked me why, I was stumped. It was the manner in which I was always taught to play defense and I never really thought about why it was done that way. Tommy made me think. "Well," I said, "I suppose it is because, with your palms up, you have less of a chance of being called for a reaching foul."

"Coach," Tommy responded, "I won't reach." Tommy had better balance with his palms down. He had a tremendous knack for stopping the dribbler and, therefore, became a National Defensive Player of the Year and the best on-the-ball defender Duke has ever had. He instinctively did not reach where others may have had a tendency to do so. So why not let him do what was more natural to him? As a result, I examined with more scrutiny the way I taught other parts of the game. The lesson I learned was that, with great players, it pays to be flexible. There isn't just one way to do things.

Six years later, I had another great defender on my team named Grant Hill. He was the most graceful player I have ever coached. He had a great career at Duke, was an All-America, and the National Defensive Player of the Year. After graduating, he became the third overall pick in the 1994 NBA draft.

Grant had a different way of denying the ball to the player he was guarding. Though I had always taught that this should be done with a fully extended arm, Grant did not completely extend his. I asked him why, and he said that he felt more comfortable doing it that way. He was great at denying the ball, and if he felt more comfortable doing it that way, then that's the way he should do it. He got the job done, and he got it done extremely well.

From that day at practice with Tommy in 1983, I learned that the things you teach do not necessarily apply to everyone in every situation. And it was a lesson I had learned from an eighteen-year-old freshman point guard! Learning from your students is something a teacher in class may be able to do by asking them questions and allowing them to participate. Interaction between the coach and the player, the teacher and the student, or the parent and the child is the best way for both parties to learn.

I always remind myself that you learn forever and from everyone. That is why, with everyone I meet, I try to listen with an open mind and the willingness to learn. You never know when or from whom your next great lesson will come!

Love

In 1974, when I was twenty-seven, my wife, Mickie, and I took a big chance and gave up the steady income and benefits of my being an Army captain with five years of experience to pursue a career as a basketball coaching family.

The situation was a difficult one for a young family. With our four-year-old daughter, Debbie, we moved to Bloomington, Indiana, where I become a graduate assistant at Indiana University. In addition to attending classes and studying, a graduate assistant's duties were the same as a full-time assistant, including going on the road to recruit. As a result, I was away from home literally every weekend. Mickie had a job at a local bank in order to supplement our income and was also working hard raising Debbie. It was difficult for us to find time to spend as a family, and many times we felt very distant from one another.

One evening when I returned home after a recruiting trip, my wife and I began a discussion about *us*. "What is going on? What is this about?" she asked, in reference to our current situation. "We are always apart. You don't spend time with us. Why are we even married? Why are we doing this?" she said. Her questions really bothered me, and, distraught, I put my head in my hands.

"I don't know," I responded. "It must be love."

After a slight pause, Mickie burst out with laughter and I burst out with relief. I had given the right answer, the only answer. Then the two of us laughed together. "I think you're right," she said.

For me, that story is a reminder that love does not always make sense, nor is it always convenient. Even when circumstances were seemingly against us, Mickie and I always told ourselves and each other that we had to work hard to keep love strong and to nurture it. We believe that love and marriage is, above all else, about making each other better.

The two of us have spent thirty-seven years together, and as our family increased to include three daughters, we learned that love grows as our family does. As our girls have grown older, each of them has fallen in love and married. In their choice of spouses, my wife and I have asked them only one question. Do you make each other better? In all three cases, they responded with an enthusiastic "Yes!" And they were right. All three of my sons-in-law have made my daughters better, and in turn, my daughters have made them better, the same way Mickie and I have always done.

As your family becomes larger, showing love may become less convenient because of the many responsibilities and often conflicting schedules. But we have always sought ways to express our love for one another, whether those means are conventional or out of the ordinary.

Because Mickie and I have that foundation of love and the love has grown to include our daughters and their families, we are able to extend our love to a larger group, the Duke Basketball family. I love each of my assistants and players, and so do my wife and daughters. With them, just like with my wife and family, we have to work on our relationships and find ways to express our love for one another. When times are difficult, when I experience setbacks, and when I want to ask why I am even doing this, I tell myself *it must be love.*

Motivation

Motivation: the extra push needed to reach a goal.

You can't just write out a game plan of how to motivate people, you have to do it by feel. You have to know your people.

One of the best ways to motivate is to be sure that you have surrounded yourself with great teammates. I think my mom explained it the best. As I was walking out the door of our inner-city Chicago home on my first day of high school, she told me, *"Mike, be sure that you get on the right bus."*

"Mom, I know what bus to take. Damen to Armitage or Division to Grand—"

"No, that's not what I mean," she said. She went on to explain that I was starting high school and that I would meet many people and learn many new things. She wanted me to make sure that I chose the right people to get on my figurative bus. And she did not want me to get on the bus of anyone who would lead me in the wrong direction. In other words, she meant for me to be on great teams.

I have been lucky to be on some tremendous teams in my life: the United States Army, Duke University, my church, and my family. I have found that great teams serve to motivate me as an individual.

When you are on a bus with good people, you and those people are mutually motivated simply by being around one another. There is an atmosphere and an attitude conducive to winning.

Once you feel confident that you are on the right bus, the next step is establishing great relationships with the people around you. For my team, this begins in the recruiting process. We do not over-recruit and are very choosy when offering a scholarship. In fact, in all of my twenty-six seasons at Duke, we have never once utilized our full allotment of scholarships. Sometimes by adding more in terms of quantity, you actually get less in terms of team cohesiveness and the ability to form relationships. We seek young men who have talent, of course, but also those who possess the values and qualities necessary to be part of a team, young men who we believe will share in our vision. Young men of character.

The development of these relationships takes

time. There is time spent working on the fundamentals of basketball and teaching them our team offensive and defensive concepts, but there is also time spent talking to one another, goofing with one another, and sharing moments off the court. People tell you things in different ways and a leader's job is to learn that where one individual may sit down and say, "Coach, I am really down right now," another may say it with a facial expression, their body language, or merely with their eyes. There are countless different ways of communicating. And I have to learn to respond to each. One of the most fascinating things about leading is figuring out how different people communicate their emotions. My goal is to learn, for each kid and for the team as a whole, how to recognize what they are attempting to communicate. I get better as a coach as I learn to respond in a quicker and more effective manner.

Once you come to know and understand the people on your bus as individuals, you will also come to realize that everyone needs to be motivated differently. There is no specific formula. I motivate by feel. There are times for patting on the back, times for hugging, and times for yelling. I don't give my teams an inspirational *Braveheart*-like speech in the locker room before every single game. Sometimes you can look in their eyes and see that they are already prepared to play. In other words, motivating people must be a flexible and versatile process. And you have to know the people on your bus well enough to see which tactics to apply at what times. I follow my heart in these situations. I instinctively react to the needs of the individual or the team.

Even as a coach and a leader, I will not always drive the bus. At times, I have to let others take the wheel. Maybe there is nothing I can say to my team before a game that will get them in the right frame of mind, but there may be something that Steve Wojciechowski can say as an assistant coach, or something that Chris Duhon can say as a team captain. No one person can be the sole source of a team's motivation. Everybody on the bus feeds off one another's excitement, belief, and commitment to the team.

Over the years I have been motivated by what a player says or the look on his face. In the locker room before a game, I might be nervous as I walk in to talk to my team. When I see David, Billy, Tommy, Danny, Tony, Trajan, Chris, and countless others sitting at the edge of their chairs in great anticipation of competing, it always motivates me to be a better leader. *When we motivate each other, our bus usually ends up at a great destination.*

Next Play

In basketball and in life, I have always maintained the philosophy of "next play." Essentially, what it means is that *whatever you have just done is not nearly as important as what you are doing right now.*

The "next play" philosophy emphasizes the fact that the most important play of the game or life moment on which you should always focus is the next one. It is not about the turnover I committed last time down the court, it's not even about the three-pointer I hit to tie the game, it is about what's next. To waste time lamenting a mistake or celebrating a success is distracting and can leave you and your team unprepared for what you are about to face. It robs you of the ability to do your best at that moment and to give your full concentration. It's why I love basketball. Plays happen with rapidity and there may be no stop-action. Basketball is a game that favors the quick thinker and the person who can go on to the next play the fastest.

It is the same in life. If one of my daughters brought home a bad grade on a report card, of course my wife and I would be concerned and feel compelled to take action. However, it is fruitless to continue to harp on what she should have done last semester to raise her grade. That is all in the past. The grade is what it is and will remain as such. However, it becomes imperative to focus on what's next: the next homework assignment, the next study session she can attend, the next test. These upcoming events grant the opportunity for improvement, that the next report card could show an A. If we work together to focus on this next play, we will all feel good that we have addressed the problem and not merely bemoaned what we should or could have done in the past.

In our basketball season, the ultimate moment for "next play" is March Madness, tournament time. At this point, I always tell my team, "Okay, as of right now, we are 0–0," meaning all of our wins and losses, any praise or criticism we have received, all individual performances and honors mean nothing now. All that matters is the journey on which we are about to embark.

This past 2006 season, before the Atlantic Coast Conference and NCAA tournaments, my staff and I needed to find an impactful way to emphasize our collective need to move on to the next play. We had a great regular season and ended up 27–3, we were No. 3 in the national polls, and were the ACC regular season champs. Additionally, two of our players, J.J. Redick and Shelden Williams, had tremendous seasons in which they broke numerous individual records and were given constant media attention as two of the best players in the country. However, we had just come off two of the worst weeks of basketball that we had played all year, with back-to-back conference losses against Florida State and North Carolina. We were very distracted.

The first part of our plan was to change venues, to get out of the locker room and the gym and meet somewhere comfortable, intimate, and, most importantly, different. We scheduled our team meal and meeting in one of the banquet rooms at the nearby Washington Duke Inn. After our meal, we conducted a thorough analysis of the tape of our last game against UNC. We got out a chalkboard and created two columns: good plays and bad plays. The motivation behind this was that we wanted to get a really good look at who we were as a team at that particular time. Once we finished reviewing the tape, our managers brought out two large cardboard boxes, one labeled "Preseason NIT," and the other "Regular Season."

I told my team that we were going to fill the boxes with everything that had come before this moment in time. At the beginning of the season, our team had won the NIT championship. So in that box we put the trophy from that tournament, all-tournament team and MVP plaques of our individual players, and the tapes of the games. In the "Regular Season" box we did the same, filling it with scouting reports and game tapes from our regular season games. I then asked each member of the team to write down on a piece of paper anything that they wanted to include: memories and frustrations from the season to that point, individual honors they had received, anything that they felt should be included relating to their personal experiences in our season. The personal statements were sealed in envelopes marked with each player's name and placed in the box.

"Okay," I said, "when we close these boxes, we are 0–0. We have had a great season to this point and have many things to be proud of. But that is not for right now. At the end of our season, we will open these boxes, return your envelopes to each of you, and collectively remember and recognize all that we have done together. But for right now, it's on to the next play."

We won the ACC Tournament, another out-
standing team accomplishment, especially considering that only five teams in the past twenty years
have won both the outright regular season championship and the ACC Tournament championship.
They have all been Duke teams. Again, something
to celebrate. But not now. After we returned to
Durham and the brackets for the NCAA tournament were revealed, our staff brought out another
box labeled "ACC Tournament." We filled that box,
sealed it, and put it away.

Bringing out a final empty box, this one labeled
"NCAA Tournament," I asked my team to imagine
the things that we could put into this box. The next
day, we would begin preparing for our first NCAA
tournament game against Southern University. Next
play.

Ownership

Whatever we have, let's take care of it.

My mom was a person of modest means. But everything she had, she valued. One day, getting off of a city bus in Chicago, she was attacked by three young men who tried to take her purse away from her. They knocked her down and pulled at her purse but she never surrendered it. The young men, seeing other people approaching, ran away. Afterward, my brother and I asked my mom, "Why didn't you just give them the purse? They could have hurt you." Her only response was, "It's my purse. It didn't belong to them."

I learned about ownership from both my mom and the neighborhood in which I grew up. It was not affluent or ritzy, but it was a great place to grow up because everyone took the time and effort to take care of it. Every day, I would see people planting flowers or sweeping the sidewalks, doing whatever they could to improve the community because they felt ownership of it. Watching the adults around me care for our neighborhood established a great foundation for me. I learned that if something belongs to me, I should take good care of it.

At Duke, my staff and I try to create a climate where everyone believes it is theirs. When our players, managers, and staff feel ownership they feel empowered and proud. But, most importantly, they feel inspired to take care of the program, uphold its standards, and defend its beliefs.

Often a leader feels as if he has to be in control of everything taking place on his or her team. I want my philosophy of leadership to create a much greater sense of ownership among all members of the team.

Picture your team as a wagon wheel and you, the leader, as its hub. The spokes of the wheel run from the people on the outer rim to the leader at the center, representing the relationships that the leader forms with each member of the team. If this is how your team is modeled, imagine what happens to the wheel when the hub is removed. Without the leader, the entire team will collapse.

Because I believe in making my teams stronger than any one individual, including myself as the leader, I have learned to operate in a different and

much more effective way. Instead of having all relationships run directly to me, I have placed an em-
phasis on forming bonds among *all* members of the
team. Now the spokes do not merely run from player
to head coach but rather from player to player, assistant to player, manager to assistant, and so on.
These relationships will sustain the wheel even if its
hub is removed. The wheel is sustained by mutual
ownership, not by a single individual serving as the
wheel's hub. We all do a better job of taking care of
what's ours when we feel as if the ownership is dis-
tributed equally.

The team belongs to all of us and it is the responsibility of all of us to sustain it and to defend its
values, purely because they are ours.

OWNERSHIP IN ACTION

One of my favorite cheers performed by our
students and the rest of the "Cameron Crazies" in
our home arena, Cameron Indoor Stadium, is a
simple chant in which they merely repeat, "Our
house . . . our house . . . our house!!!" Many students even have T-shirts that state this simple
message.

Our students actually feel like they are part of
the team. They are not entertained by the team,
they are on the team, it's theirs. They are truly our
"sixth man." The message, "Our House," is that we

need to protect what is ours. Our players, our staff, and our students have an obligation to Duke University to do whatever we do with the utmost pride and intensity. The chant is a reminder that in our house, under our collective roof, we need to defend what belongs to us.

I want to create an atmosphere in which everyone feels a part of the team and knows that they are important. They are! When everyone has this feeling of ownership, our wheel will never collapse.

Passion

When I have speaking engagements, I often tell my audience how lucky I am to have never had a job. After some confused laughter, I explain that, because I have always done what I love to do, I have never considered my work a job. I have merely been pursuing my passion and loving every minute of it.

I define passion as extreme emotion. When you are passionate, you always have your destination in sight and you are not distracted by obstacles. Because you love what you are pursuing, things like rejection and setbacks will not hinder you in your pursuit. You believe that nothing can stop you!

A key question in leading, and particularly in parenting, is: how do I discover what my child is passionate about? My advice would be to allow a young person to try as many things as they can: science, history, sports, music, art, writing. Allow them to attempt a number of things and then simply watch for their eyes to light up. I knew my daughter Lindy had a passion for theater from looking into her eyes after her first play, just like I knew Steve Wojciechowski's passion for leadership after watching him in one of his high school games. It is vital that you allow people to discover their own passions.

My passion has been for teaching and coaching, from the days when I organized my buddies into teams in a Chicago schoolyard, to acting as a player-coach on a post basketball team while serving in the Army, to having the opportunity to coach some of the world's elite athletes as the United States National Team coach. One of the reasons I have been able to achieve some of these things is that I never kept my passion to myself. I told my parents what I loved to do early on in life, and as a result, they were supportive of the decisions I made, even when they did not completely understand. Additionally, I have always shared my goals with my wife, Mickie, and she has been my most important teammate throughout our marriage and career. Sharing your passion with those who love you can provide you with the support you need to overcome obstacles along the way. Likewise, it is vital that you be supportive of the passions of those whom you love, particularly your spouse and children.

Additionally, in putting together a team, it is important that the leader not be the sole passion-provider for that team. You have to find others who feel the same way you do. This is one reason I surround myself with assistant coaches who are equally motivated. During videotape sessions and scouting reports that often last all night, my assistants and I continually find strength and inspiration in each other's drive toward our common goal. Surrounding yourself with other passionate people can help keep you motivated and driven.

PASSION IN ACTION

No one who has heard one of his broadcasts can deny Dick Vitale's passion for the game of basketball. I was surprised when I learned that Dick had begun his career as an accountant following his graduation from Seton Hall with a business degree. But for him, accounting was his job, not his passion. So he took a great risk in pursuing a coaching career and was initially met with many letters of rejection. However, because he never stopped listening to his passion and had the support of his family, Dick eventually landed a coaching spot at an elementary school. His passion continued to lead him to the high school coaching ranks, then to college, and even to the NBA before he became a broadcaster with ESPN. Dick has indicated to me that the reason behind his success in broadcasting is the fact that he's never really felt like a broadcaster. He approaches the game with the passion of a player and a coach, and as a result he feels the necessary empathy for those he discusses on television. His contagious passion, quite frankly, is why he is the best in the business.

My friend Jim Valvano was one of the most passionate people I have ever known. College basketball fans may remember his celebratory run, arms extended, across the court after North Carolina State's last-second victory to win the National Championship in 1983. But Jimmy's legacy extends well beyond the boundary lines of the basketball court.

When Jimmy was diagnosed with incurable cancer in 1992, he started his passionate crusade to discover a cure for the disease. Jimmy knew that he could not be saved, but he was not stymied by this fact. His passion became to beat cancer, even though he knew the victory would come after his death. He enlisted the help of many of his good friends, including myself and Dick Vitale, and he acted on his passion along with the passions of his teammates by starting the Jimmy V Foundation for Cancer Research. To date, the foundation has raised over $50 million and is now fully endowed. Jimmy V's legacy is a legacy of passion. And now it is up to those of us on the foundation board, contributors, and those doctors and scientists who are passionate about what they do to finish what Jimmy started.

Anytime I need to put in perspective what passion is really all about, I watch the tape of Jimmy's speech at the 1993 ESPY Awards. When he finishes with the amazing words, *"Don't give up, don't ever give up,"* I get chills remembering what true passion can empower someone to do.

Poise

P oise: keeping your composure in spite of the circumstances.

Poise requires maturity. It's about remaining mentally and emotionally balanced all the time, no matter what is taking place around you.

In competition, the element of poise can make you appear much stronger in the eyes of your opponent than can your talent alone. I tell my players that you never want to show your opponent a weakness through your words, facial expressions, or body language. No matter what they are saying to you, no matter what the crowd is chanting, if you can show poise, you demonstrate to your opponent that they cannot rattle you. Just keep your mind on what you're doing and maintain that inner balance. Act like you have been there before and that you expect to do well.

When one of our bigger players is positioned
on the offensive end of the court, near the basket, we say that he is "in the post." Many times
when this player receives the ball, he is instantly
guarded by two defenders who are trying to
double-team him. Being double-teamed creates
quite a challenge and it is hard to keep your wits
about you. On our teams, we continually use the
expression with our post players that they must
show "poise in the post." This means that if you
get double-teamed, you must remain composed.
Remember your training and make a choice. Ask
yourself: What do I do? Do I pass the ball out to
a teammate? Do I make a move to the basket? Do
not panic. Make a play.

The opposite of poise is panic, and if your opponent sees that, they will double-team you time
and time again. If you can maintain composure,
though, your opponent's best efforts are foiled.
They will see that they have not succeeded in
robbing you of your poise and they will know that
they cannot dictate your reaction.

Likewise, as a guard, you can find yourself facing full-court pressure defense, or being trapped
by defenders in one of the corners of the court.
Do you let panic set in and turn the ball over?
Again, remember your training and make a
choice. Do you call timeout? Or can you see past

the trap to an open teammate who is prepared to score?

In moments of doubt, I tell my players to listen to that voice inside their head and to be sure that the voice is always positive. It's the one that says things like, "I'm good" and "I can do this." Tune out the voice that says things like, "Oh no" and "I'm really in trouble, here." If you make a habit of this, that negative voice will eventually disappear entirely.

When you are able to show poise as an individual, you set an example for others of how to handle a tough situation. This is why, even in stressful game situations, I try to never let my team see fear or defeat on my face. I want to show them, through my own actions, the path to success. I want to show them that I've been there before.

There come times when it is necessary for you and your team to show poise together. When the game is on the line and one play will decide whether you win or lose, the team that exhibits maturity and poise has the greatest chance of coming out victorious.

I believe that sport is a tremendous venue in which young people can develop poise. The value of sport is in using the lessons learned on the court or the playing field to help you in other aspects of your life. Poise is not about winning and losing—you can show poise and still lose a game. However, you will have a much better chance of winning if you learn how to keep your composure in spite of the circumstances.

Pressure

P ressure is a compelling influence. It can be suffocating, stifling, and can cause individuals to resort to negative action or no action at all.

When you are attempting to deal with pressure, there are some things that you can do to ensure that it does not overwhelm you and that you become better as a result of the experience.

The ability to handle pressure is all in how you look at it. I look at being put under pressure as an opportunity to show how strong and capable you and your team really are.

Preparation is key if you hope to operate well under pressure. Hopefully, during the course of your training, you have done enough thinking about what it is like to feel pressure. If you think about the potential for pressure in advance, you can use repetitions and simulations in practice to help you feel as if you have been in that spot before.

Another way to help cope with pressure is segmenting. I try to divide the situation into manageable steps rather than considering the imposing big picture. It seems much more simplistic. When it becomes a task-by-task process, the big picture will not cause overwhelming pressure. When one of my basketball teams goes into the NCAA Tournament, we do just that. If I went into the locker room and said, "Okay, here is what we need to do. We need to win six games and become National Champions," that would put an undue amount of pressure on the team. Instead, I tell them to focus on one game at a time and to segment the NCAAs into three two-game tournaments. If we win our first two games, we go to the Sweet Sixteen, if we win our next two, we go to the Final Four, and if we win the next two, we are National Champions. Each of those segments becomes a four-team tournament that we have to win in order to advance, and that is much less intimidating.

In addition, if you have built a great support group around you, you know that the pressure is not yours to deal with on your own. Therefore, another part of segmenting is dividing up responsibility among members of your team. This past year, we had an end-of-game pressure situation on our home court against Virginia Tech. With 1.6 seconds left on the clock, we were down by one point and needed to go full-court and score in order to win the game. Josh McRoberts's responsibility was to get the ball inbounds. Sean Dockery's part was to catch the ball and shoot. Our staff had put the play together. The players on the bench and students in the stands needed to provide support and keep the level of intensity high. That way, each member of the team was able to focus on a specific task rather than on the big picture, which was: we had a heck of a lot to do in a very short amount of time in order to win. But everyone maintained the understanding that we are a part of a team, and in this pressure situation each player just had to do his part and trust that the others would do the same. As a result of this segmenting of responsibility, Sean Dockery was able to hit a three-pointer from just across half-court and we won the game 77–75!

Ultimately, having pressure on you is a healthy thing. If you are never put in pressure situations, you are not testing your limits and you will never see how far you can go. You are just playing it safe. And remember, for those times you do not succeed under the pressure, if you do not hit that last-second shot, you should never consider yourself a failure. You should feel proud that you have done your very best in a tough situation. Even when it feels like the pressure is on, *never fear the result of your best effort.* Just concentrate on making the play.

PRESSURE IN ACTION

In all my years of coaching, no player has handled pressure more gracefully than Christian Laettner. A two-time National Champion, one of the only players in history to play in four Final Fours, 1992 National Player of the Year, and the all-time NCAA Tournament leader in points scored, Christian hit more pressure shots than anyone I have ever coached: a last-second shot against Connecticut his sophomore year to send us to the 1990 Final Four, two free throws against UNLV his junior season that led us to the 1991 National Championship, and the incredible last-second shot versus Kentucky in the 1992 East Regional final that will live forever in the memories of basketball fans.

Christian thrived under pressure. He loved it. And now, years later, talking to him about those shots reminds me of how I must continue to coach my future teams to operate under pressure. When I asked him how he was able to handle pressure so well, he said to me, "Because I had a responsibility to the people around me to do my best. I always knew that the only people I had to answer to were the people in the locker room. That was my responsibility and that is why I wanted to succeed." He told me that the staff at Duke had taught him that he could be successful if he gave of himself to be a part of the team. His team was his primary motivation when he was, what he called "blessed," to be put in those pressure situations.

I marvel when I listen to Christian, because what seems so plainly simple to him is nearly impossible for others to see. But if more players can look at it the way Christian did, perhaps they can find enough strength in those around them, in their team, and in their preparation to realize that these situations really are blessings. Then they can confidently give their all and never, ever fear the result.

Pride

Pride can come from many sources, but ultimately it can be defined as self-respect and a feeling of satisfaction over an accomplishment. It can also be a feeling you get from being a part of something bigger than you.

There is a dignity that comes from doing something well or being a part of a group that does something well. Pride means having an understanding that you put your signature on everything that you do and ensuring then that what you do is done in the best manner possible.

The first person to ever teach me about pride was my mom. She told me, "Michael, everything you do has your personal signature on it. You should take pride in it because it's yours." As I have grown older, I have come to develop a better and deeper understanding of what she meant. You do not have pride in something because it earns you accolades or because someone gives you a trophy or tells you it's great. The pride comes not in the recognition you receive for something, but merely in *doing that thing to the best of your ability.* Whether you are playing a basketball game, painting a portrait, or cleaning your house, you should take deliberate pride in it because it is a reflection of you. It will always carry your signature.

But my mom didn't merely teach me pride by telling me what it means, she taught me by being an example of pride in everything she did, right down to the way she made chocolate chip cookies. No matter what day it was or who the cookies were for, she always made them the exact same way: the very best way she could. She put the utmost care and paid such attention to detail that each cookie would have an equal number of chocolate chips. When we couldn't afford much, there were three chips. Later, there were four. But they were always the same because they were *always* the best chocolate chip cookies she could make. After all, they were *hers.* Anything that Emily Krzyzewski did was going to be the best.

That type of pride is individual pride and it is vital to have in every aspect of your life. But the greatest pride of all comes from being a part of something that you could never do alone—being a part of a team. Players on a basketball team, members of a great family, troops serving in the military: those people have the potential to feel the greatest pride of all. Then, in everything you do, not only do you sign it with your personal signature, but with that of the group as a whole: Duke, the Krzyzewskis, the United States of America.

One of the proudest days of my life was when I was inducted into the Naismith Basketball Hall of Fame in 2001. While standing at the podium that day, I could not help but think of my dad. When my parents were young, times were difficult for an immigrant family with a distinctly Polish name. In order to avoid the inevitable ethnic discrimination he would experience, my dad actually shortened his name to the more acceptable William Kross. This helped him in applying for jobs and when he served as a private in the United States Army during World War II. The pride I felt at my induction was multiplied by the pride I knew my father would feel were he still living. Now the name Krzyzewski would join some of the greatest names in basketball: Erving, Russell, Knight, Smith.

To think that at one point my dad had to change his name, and now—his real name, our family name, the name we are all proud of—would be looked upon with honor and distinction. What an amazing moment!

It was the concept of collective pride that inspired my staff and me to bring our team together the evening prior to a home conference game in 2006. Typically, we all meet in the locker room for our standard pre-game meeting. This time, however, I asked them to join me on the Cameron court where the center circle is painted with the large "D" that is our Duke Basketball logo. We vowed that the next day, each of us was going to do our very best to represent ourselves with pride as individuals, the Duke team, and as defenders of our home court. Giving each member of the staff and each player a permanent marker, we all signed the "D" at center court, thus agreeing to the terms we, as a team, had established.

In signing the court that evening, we symbolized how everything we did on that court, as members of this team and as individuals, was going to be done with pride. And now it, most literally, had our signature on it. We were going to hold ourselves accountable to take care of what was ours. Nobody had the right to come into our gymnasium and take away our pride. Our house, our tradition, our Duke name meant too much to us. We would play to the best of our ability, we would uphold our standard of excellence, and we would do it together. We won that night, and in his post-game interview, Duke senior guard Sean Dockery said, "It was something where you look down there and it's your house. *Today I saw my own signature down there and said, 'Come on, you have to play hard.'* "

Pride means ensuring that anything that you do, anything that has your name on it, is done right. So for my team, anything that Duke does should be done to the highest level. I want myself, my players, and my staff to have as much pride as my mom and dad did. Remember, the effort that you use to do this is rewarded tenfold by the feeling you get from your actions.

Respect

Wen I hear the word "respect," I think
of treating everyone the same.

I had the great privilege of being an assistant
on the 1992 Olympic team, known as the "Dream
Team." It consisted of some of the greatest players
of all time, such as Michael Jordan, Magic John-
son, and Larry Bird. As a part of that team, I
learned a lot about the game, but I also relearned
a lesson about respect.

After a team practice, I stood by myself on the
sidelines drinking a Diet Coke. Michael Jordan
walked over to me and said, "Coach K, I would like
to do about a half hour of individual work and I was
wondering if you could please work with me." So
there I was, faced with a very difficult decision:
working with the greatest basketball player of all

time or continuing to drink my Diet Coke. I think I
made the right decision.

After our workout, Michael shook my hand
and said, "Thanks, Coach."

Michael Jordan had just called me "Coach,"
and he had said "please" and "thank you." This
was at a time when he was at the very top of his
game and was one of the most recognizable faces
not only in sport but throughout the world.
Michael Jordan had earned global recognition as
a symbol of excellence. That day, I learned that
everyone on Michael Jordan's team is treated with
respect.

I have said many times that my mother was
the greatest person in my life. She had an eighth-
grade education and cleaned floors at the Chicago
Athletic Club for a living. So I had the benefit of
learning at an early age that some of the greatest
people in the world clean floors for a living. When
you value everyone and treat everyone with respect, you may just be amazed at how they can
make you better.

One of my very best friends at Duke was a
custodian named D.C. Williams. He and I had a
tremendous relationship. Many people think that I
was merely being kind talking to D.C. and spending
time with him, when in reality I valued his friendship and advice as much as anyone in my life.

D.C. was responsible for the cleanliness and
upkeep of our locker room area at Duke. But in
addition to taking care of his responsibilities, he
maintained a spirit that permeated through everyone in our program. You knew when D.C. was
around because there would be gospel music playing and he would be diligently at work with his
ever-positive attitude.

D.C. did his job with obvious pride. Because
his standards were so high for his own work, it
raised everyone else's standards as well. Our players wouldn't want to drop something on the floor
knowing that D.C. would have to pick it up. D.C.
helped to create an atmosphere conducive to success, one with the bar set high and drenched in
pride.

During his eighteen years at Duke, it was
D.C.'s locker room, not Coach K's locker room,
or Grant Hill's locker room, or Shane Battier's
locker room. D.C. took ownership and everyone
benefited as a result. Often he would offer insight
into the mood of the team or a particular player
based on his observations. "Coach, something is
not right with Nate," or "I think the team is really
down this week." I would always listen. And he was
always right.

We have had a great winning percentage on
our home court during the past couple of decades.

When I walk off the court at the completion of each home game, I do not stop to talk or shake hands with anyone; I am focused on getting to my team in the locker room. But after every home game for eighteen years, the person that I did shake hands with was D.C. He was always in the same spot waiting for me. Win or lose, D.C. was my true friend. And, like any true friend, he made me better.

I spoke at D.C.'s funeral in 2005 and had the privilege of meeting some of his family and friends. I was told over and over about how proud D.C. was to be a part of Duke. Additionally, I was instantly validated in the eyes of everyone there, because D.C. had had respect for me as well. Imagine all we would have missed out on if we had not initially shown respect for one another.

Too often, people will miss out on meaningful relationships with amazing people because they quickly pass judgment based on what that person does for a living, the clothes they wear, what kind of car they drive. D.C. Williams was a great man. I miss him terribly. But I was lucky to have known him and to have benefited from our eighteen-year friendship. I would never have received all of those benefits had I not initially treated him with respect and understood how important it is to value everyone. The simple act of showing respect can allow you to meet people like D.C. Williams, to let them come into your life, and to make you a better person.

Selflessness

Selflessness means that you will do what is best for the team. Jimmy Valvano once told me, *"A person does not become whole until he or she becomes a part of something bigger than himself or herself."* It is the best and most simple description of being a member of a team and its rewards that I have ever heard.

Being a part of something bigger than yourself requires selflessness and an understanding that there will be personal sacrifice for the good of the team. And most people desire to be a part of something bigger and to feel as if their actions are for the greater good.

Non-scholarship players, known as "walk-ons," have always been an important part of our program, serving as an ideal illustration of selflessness. They receive minimal playing time and virtually no media attention but are expected to work just as hard as any All-America. One of the greatest walk-on stories of my career came in the 2004–05 season after back-to-back losses to Maryland and Virginia Tech. I was furious with my starters and a statement needed to be made.

In a brief meeting following those losses, I announced to our team that those who had exhibited the best work ethic would be rewarded with starting positions against our upcoming opponent, Wake Forest. My staff and I thought it would be a key moment in our season, a turning point, and that it would send a message to the entire team. But what happened, thanks to the selflessness of former team manager and junior walk-on Ross Perkins, turned what we thought would be a good moment into a great one.

At our next practice, I put the names of four of our five starters on the board; they were all walk-ons. I then told my team that whoever played the hardest in practice that day would be given the fifth spot. At the end of practice, the lineup was set: four walk-ons and J.J. Redick.

A walk-on can expect to see only a few minutes of playing time throughout the course of a season, and so for a walk-on to start in a conference game has the potential to be one of the greatest days of that individual's life. After our lineup announcement, Ross Perkins asked if he could come by my office and speak with me privately. "Of course," I replied.

When Ross came in twenty minutes later, we sat down and began a great discussion. "Coach," Ross said, "when you put my name on that board, it was the proudest moment of my life."

"Ross, you deserve it. You are going to start against Wake Forest tomorrow."

What happened then changed the course of our season.

Ross looked me in the eye and said, "Coach, thank you so much for the opportunity and for having confidence in me, but I think it would be better for the team if Shelden starts tomorrow . . ." Here was a kid who truly wanted what was best for the team and was willing to give up what could have been a very memorable personal moment in order for us, together, to be successful. Amazing!

I was completely taken aback. Now the moment was no longer about my disappointment in our team's play for the past two games. Now it was about the incredible selflessness of this kid and his sacrifice of individual glory for the good of the team. Ross's actions remind us all of what it means to be a part of something bigger than you, and I will talk about Ross Perkins and his selflessness for the rest of my career.

Shelden did start against Wake Forest and we

were victorious in what was a tightly fought game. Ross was the first player I went to hug afterward. Ironically, he never played a second in that game, but his selflessness is the reason we won.

Standards

Standards: a level of excellence that we consider our norm.

After a particularly frustrating conference road loss in 2004, our second in a row, my team and I were riding back to Durham on our team bus. Typically after a loss, I have some idea of the next steps that our team needs to take. I often have a direction in mind—maybe not a solution, but at least a direction. For the first two and a half hours of the three-hour bus trip, I went through many options in my mind regarding the appropriate action to take. I finally came to the conclusion that, on this occasion, I was lost.

I said to my staff, "I have never told you this before and it may be a little scary, but I have no feelings or intuition on this one. My instincts have escaped me." I looked to my associate head coach

and longtime friend, Johnny Dawkins, and told
him that I simply did not know what to do. He
touched me on the arm and spoke some incredible
words.

"Coach," he said, in his typical calm but com-
manding and dependable tone, "*it's all about standards.*"

Johnny was absolutely right. All of a sudden, my
coaching instincts came back to me, and, along
with my staff, we developed a plan of attack. As the
bus stopped at Cameron Indoor Stadium, I asked
the team to come to the locker room for a quick
meeting. I repeated to them what Johnny had just
told me. It is not about losses; it is about standards.
We needed to be playing at the level that Duke
teams play. We were simply not doing that. As a
team, we had allowed our standards to slip. It had
become acceptable to not play every defensive possession with the utmost intensity, to allow offensive
rebounds, and to play as individuals on offense. We
thought that we could do less and still receive the
same rewards.

Standards define what is and is not acceptable
for an individual or a team. When you allow your
standards to slip, you are saying, "We do not have to
be this good all the time," and as a result your level
of success will decrease right alongside your team
effort, work ethic, and sense of pride. We made

sure that we got back to the standards we had set for ourselves.

After a very disappointing NCAA tournament loss, a close friend of mine, Steve Delmont, sent me a Jean Giraudoux quote, *"Only the mediocre are always at their best."* If your standards are low, it is easy to meet those standards every single day, every single year. But if your standard is to be the best, there will be days when you fall short of that goal. It is okay to not win every game. The only problem would be if you allow a loss or a failure to change your standards. Keep your standards intact, keep the bar set high, and continue to try your very best every day to meet those standards. If you do that, you can always be proud of the work that you do.

I am lucky to have teammates like Johnny and friends like Steve to remind me that, when it comes down to it, it's all about standards.

Talent

Talent is natural ability. It is important but it isn't everything.

A team is a collection of individuals with varying levels of talent. When you talk about talent in the context of a team, you can talk about it both individually and collectively. The more talent you and your team have, the more room for error. I often employ the analogy that talent is really the difference between taking a superhighway and having to take side streets to reach a destination. In other words, if you have a lot of talent, the road is wider, it is easier. You can get to your destination faster if you do it the right way. But even if you do not have a lot of talent, you can still reach your destination. There are more obstacles, and therefore I refer to operating with less talent as taking side streets. The lanes are not as wide. You may have to be more creative and innovative, and it probably will take more time and effort.

One of the key things to remember about talent is that it has to be developed. When you've got it, it's like having amazing raw materials. But those raw materials do not become anything of substance unless they are honed through hard work and learning. Developing your talents makes you strong. If you only use your raw talent, it can eventually make you weak by allowing you to merely "get by." You can even lose your talent because it has not been developed. The road can come to an abrupt end.

The maturing process is a key factor in the development of talent, and education is a major part of becoming a mature adult: education in the classroom, on the court, and in life. That is why school is a great venue for the development of talent. In school, an individual is educated in all facets of life. They are tested in every way. Places like Duke are amazing because you are around excellence all the time, and being around excellence makes you strive to be better.

Chris Carrawell is a great example of talent development. When he came to Duke from inner-city St. Louis, he was intelligent and very streetwise. In basketball, he was not the most gifted athlete, but he understood the game and how to work with his teammates to produce positive results. He was never the most talented player on my teams at Duke but he used his abilities to fit in with our star players. As a result, he kept getting better. And in his senior year, he was named the ACC Conference Player of the Year, even though he was not as physically gifted as some others in our conference. He traveled on side streets wisely and creatively to reach a destination others in the league could not reach even though they were on superhighways.

There will be times in basketball when you are matched up against an opponent with considerably less talent than you. For instance, in the first round of the NCAA Tournament, many of college basketball's best teams are matched up against teams that are simply not as talented. Our goal in those games is not just to win, but to work harder and to outplay that team. What we are trying to do is to keep developing as a basketball team. We are trying to get better so that we do not lose the talents that we have as individuals and as a team.

Many people are confused when my team has won a game by a large margin and I am still upset and disappointed by our performance. I feel that way because many times we have only won the game because of our talent. If that is the case, then we have not gotten any better as a team by playing in that game. We coasted. And getting by on talent alone is not acceptable. If we continue to rely on our talent to win games, eventually someone will be better than we are. When two equally talented teams are matched up against each other, most often the team that works harder and works together will be victorious. But never fear the talent of your opponent. You can find yourself in the position to beat a more talented team if you make up for the difference in talent with hard work and the development of a cohesive unit.

Championship teams are not always a collection of the most talented individuals. In other words, you do not need three leading actors to have a great movie, you need supporting actors as well. Our teams often have several role players who complement our most talented players. These players may not score the most points but their contribution to our team's success is not measured by statistics, it is measured in the wins and losses we achieve as a team. Often, with time and maturity, those supporting actors, like Chris Carrawell, develop into stars themselves.

Talent is a natural gift and it is a wonderful thing to have. The ability to develop your talent is a talent in itself. Whether we get to our destination on a superhighway or a side street is not the issue. The people who reach their destinations are the ones who develop their talents fully and effectively. *A talent is a blessing*, and it is our responsibility to develop it.

Trust

Trust is an enormous word if you want to live a happy, fulfilling, and productive life. As much as it means to relationships, trust should be an eighteen-syllable word. But that one syllable, those five letters, represent the foundation upon which relationships must be based, whether those relationships be one-on-one, with a team, in a business, or in a family.

Trust is developed through open and honest communication and, once established, creates a shared vision for a common goal. Established trust among a group of individuals bolsters a feeling of confidence that only comes in knowing that you are not alone. In basketball, if you are defending an offensive player on the wing and that player is able to drive past you, you have two choices: one, you can foul that player, or two, you can trust that your teammate will be there to help play defense. On our teams, we prefer the latter. As a result of this trust, you play defense with tenacious abandon. Trust brings you together and makes everyone more confident.

Trusting relationships serve as a reminder that you are not doing it alone, that someone else believes in you and that you can believe in them. If you are wondering whether or not you can "get it done" and someone you trust tells you that they believe in you—that is a powerful thing. Will you always get it done? No, but you certainly have a better chance when you possess the confidence that comes with knowing that you are not doing it alone.

Part of building trusting relationships is confrontation. I do not define confrontation as something negative; it simply means meeting the truth, head-on. In my relationships, I want you to believe me when I tell you that you are great *and* I want you to believe me when I tell you that you are not working hard enough. Both of these are confrontations, but, because we trust each other, we know that our confrontations are truthful. No time is wasted trying to decipher meaning or understand motive. The confrontation, whether the subject is positive or negative, can immediately inspire action producing a positive result.

At least once a season, I turn to one of my players in the locker room and ask them, "Son, are two
better than one?" He'll look back at me, afraid to
give the simple answer, thinking I will use the opportunity to goof on him. "Come on," I say, "it's a
simple question. Are two better than one?" Be-
grudgingly, he will eventually respond, "Yes, Coach,
of course two is better than one." "Not necessarily,"
I reply. "Two are better than one only if two can act
as one." Establishing trust among a team allows you
to act as one.

*Trust is a confident belief in your team, a person in
your life, or a member of your family.* Essentially, it
means, "I have your back." I have yours and I
believe that you have mine. Trust builds confidence, and with confidence, you and your team
have a much greater chance of achieving at a
high level.

TRUST IN ACTION

Elton Brand is a Los Angeles Clipper, an NBA
All-Star, and a member of the United States National Team. In 1998, he had just completed his
freshman year at Duke, in which we had had a great
season, losing in the NCAA Regional championship game to the University of Kentucky. At the
end of each season, many of the great players in
college basketball are pursued by the NBA to forgo

the rest of their college career and enter their name in the NBA draft.

In discussing his predicted position in the draft, Elton and I came to the conclusion that it would be better for him to come back for his sophomore year, continue his education, become a better player, and improve his position for the 1999 draft. On the last day that an undergraduate was permitted to turn in his name for the draft, I received a phone call from Elton. Because the school year had ended, he was already at home in New York. Through his tears, he explained to me that he was being pressured by many around him to enter the NBA draft and that, based on our previous discussion, this was not what he wanted to do. Instead of faltering under the pressure, Elton trusted me enough to let me know that he was feeling pulled in another direction and to ask for my guidance. In the face of a personal crisis, he came to me because we had established a basis of trust and he knew that I wanted what was best for him. Should he do what other people were asking him to do or should he do what he believed was right for him?

By the end of the day, Elton Brand was still a Duke Blue Devil. He felt strong enough to say no to the NBA. To me, he just said, "Thanks, Coach."

That summer, Elton became a key member of the United States Goodwill Basketball Team, enhancing both his skills and his reputation. Before the start of the 1998–99 season, it was predicted by many that he would be selected as the National Player of the Year.

Elton started the year playing fairly well, but not to the level that both he and I knew he could. I asked him to meet with me individually in my office, and we had a very serious talk in which I told him that he would not be in the starting lineup for our next two games. The morning after our conversation, Elton knocked on my office door, stuck his head in, and said, "Coach, you're right. And we won't have to have this talk in the future." Again, he trusted me.

At the end of the 1999 season, Elton *was* named National Player of the Year and our team had the opportunity to play in the National Championship game. This time, after the season, he and I, together with his mother, made the decision that it was the right time for him to put his name into the NBA draft. Elton became the number one overall pick in the 1999 NBA draft. He is now the go-to guy for the Los Angeles Clippers and is financially secure for the rest of his life. If you asked Elton Brand, he would tell you: *trust pays off.*

Will

E ven after reviewing the stat sheet and seeing that he had scored only one point, I knew that
Wojo had won the game; *he willed it.*

Steve Wojciechowski, nicknamed Wojo, was our
captain and senior point guard for the 1997–98
season. It was our final home game and we were
playing our archrivals, the University of North
Carolina. The winner would be the Atlantic Coast
Conference regular season champions. By our standards, the Duke program had been down the past
couple of seasons and we were just beginning to get
back on track. Since 1993, we were 1–9 against Carolina and they had a very talented team again this
year. Needless to say, we wanted this one badly, especially Wojo. This was his last game in Cameron
Indoor Stadium and he was determined that his
senior class would go out as winners.

In fact, the team wanted to win so badly that it seemed to make us play tight in the first half. We were not playing to win, we were playing not to lose, and as a result we were down by 13 at the half. At halftime, I was very emotional with my team in the locker room; I asked if they were scared and why we weren't fighting. I knew, looking into Wojo's eyes, we would play a tremendous second half, and that the outcome of the game would rely on this kid's will.

The tide began to shift at around the 12-minute mark of the second half, and by the time there were eight minutes left in the game, it felt as if the momentum had swung in our direction. It was the loudest (and the hottest) that I can remember Cameron Indoor Stadium ever being. The crowd was exceptional, Elton Brand and Roshown McLeod had begun to hit shots, and our defense had begun to slow Carolina down. It was as if our community had come together to win this game; we had to win this game. In the middle of it was Wojo; he was the maestro of it all. His job was to ensure that all of us sustained that level of intensity for the remainder of the game.

According to him, "It was one of those games where you'd rather die than lose." When you invest in something at such a high level, you will do anything to make it happen. To Wojo, there was only one possible outcome of that game. And to achieve that outcome, someone had to have the will to lead our entire community for those final eight minutes. Will begins with a foundation of character, values, and standards. As a leader or parent, you cannot merely look at a kid and order him or her to have willpower. You have to begin by establishing a core set of values that will make up his or her character. The definition of will, then, is a refusal to give up those values. Will can only be displayed when it is tested by challenging circumstances. Wojo had the will, and the UNC game that year gave him the platform on which to exhibit that will. We came back from a 17-point deficit in the second half to win 77–75, in one of the most dramatic comebacks ever in Cameron Indoor Stadium.

Many people have seen the conclusion of that game when Wojo runs across the court to me and we hug. That hug was one of the great moments of both of our careers. The reason why the two of us instinctively came together at that moment was because we both knew why we had won: he knew it and I knew it and, chances are, no one else did. We won because of Wojo's will.

Work

Ambition alone is not enough. That ambition must be coupled with hard work for success to be achieved.

I love hard work. It is a staple of all that I do and all that I ask of my teams. A lot of people hear the words "hard work" and say, "Oh, no. I don't want to do that." I want to coach kids who hear that they are going to have to work hard and then get excited about how much they will improve as a result.

I grew up in an environment of hard work. My father was an elevator operator in Chicago and my mother scrubbed floors at night at the Chicago Athletic Club. Even if they were sick or tired, they always went to work and worked hard. They truly believed that there was a dignity in their work. I attended Catholic schools my whole life, and then

West Point, where the lesson was reinforced by my teachers and coaches.

Work is a necessity if you want to improve. It is the road you have to follow to become better. Throughout my time as a coach, it is no coincidence that my best players have been the hardest workers. When I had the opportunity to serve as an assistant coach for the 1992 Olympic "Dream Team," I noticed that even these individuals, some of the greatest athletes in the world, always put forth extra effort. Players like David Robinson, Karl Malone, and Chris Mullin always had a daily routine that they did in addition to our normal practice session. They would lift weights early in the morning, work on their endurance, or stay after practice to get in extra shooting. They embraced work as the process that you go through to become exceptional.

I often give my players quotes about a certain word or topic in order to help them better understand and remember its meaning. One of my favorite quotes about hard work was said by one of the greatest coaches of all time, John Wooden. He said, *"Nothing will work unless you do."* In other words, you can have the best plans, the most perfect offensive and defensive schemes, and even a great amount of talent. But if you and your team are not willing to put in hard work, your plans will never be realized.

Another quote I often share with my players was by NBA legend Jerry West. He said, "*You don't get much done if you only work on the days that you feel good.*" Hard work cannot be sporadic. It cannot take place only on the sunny days. If you want your best to become a habit, you must engage in intensive, intelligent, and persistent practice. I believe you play like you practice, so when you practice hard every day, playing hard will seem natural when the game is on the line.

A final quote about work that I share with my teams is Roger Staubach's: "*Spectacular achievements are always preceded by unspectacular preparation.*" Hard work is not pretty, or glamorous, or even fun. But, as I learned from my coach Bob Knight, winners prepare to win. Of course, everybody would like to win. But real winners put forth the time and effort to make it happen. And, in fact, by putting in the work, you make yourself worthy of winning. And I truly believe that you will not win consistently unless you are worthy.

I have been blessed to coach some extremely hardworking young men over the years. When I coached Bobby Hurley, he would work incredibly hard throughout practice, and afterward he would get on a StairMaster and work out at least an additional half hour. He never wanted his body to tell his mind that he was tired.

Shelden Williams and J.J. Redick are the two most recent examples of what you can become by working hard all the time. Each of them never missed a practice and would never substitute themselves out of a drill. They wanted to be in every play. They also worked after practice each day to get better. Although they were ambitious, they knew that ambition alone would not do it for them. *Hard work had to form a partnership with ambition* for them to achieve the success they desired.

Conclusion
The Fist

You should never stop learning to own words. There are always more words, deeper meanings, and more stories to go with those words. Each time I witness one of these words in action, I come to own it more completely. In this book, I have offered you a beginning: forty words, explanations, and stories that are important in my life.

Coming to understand and own each individual word is a great beginning. But just as words come together to form sentences, paragraphs, and entire books, the concepts behind the words come together to form an individual's character or the collective character of a team, business, or family. For many years, I have used the analogy of The Fist to describe how five vital words come together and help to create teamwork. The Fist is a teaming of words and concepts in order to form one single powerful entity.

Five fingers held together in a tight formation, a fist, is far more effective and powerful than five fingers held outstretched and alone.

In basketball, the five individuals on the court must act as one, as a fist, in order to achieve the success that they could not find acting as five independent players.

Each separate finger that makes up The Fist symbolizes a fundamental quality that renders a team great. For my teams, we emphasize five words, all of which appear in this book: communication, trust, collective responsibility, care, and pride. I believe that any of these traits alone is important. But all five together are tough to beat. In reality, those five fingers can represent any five words that one wishes to emphasize with their team, business, or family. What unites you? What are your common purposes? And what methods do you plan to use in bringing your team together? What words comprise your Fist?

My goal, when I teach The Fist, is five people playing together for one purpose. In our pre-game and pre-practice huddles, we do not say, "Defense!" or "Win!" Instead, in unison, we say, "Together!" And we intend to play that way. The Fist serves as a symbol of how we can achieve that togetherness.

Instead of giving high fives or patting one another on the back, my teams put their fists together. When I show them my fist and they show me theirs, we remind one another of the five words that will bring us together and allow us to be the strongest that we can be.

Everyone should be able to write a book like this, illustrating the words that are important to who we are using stories from our own lives. Actually, this book does not have an ending. There are always more words, more stories and examples, and heightened understanding. There are words that others could teach me that I do not yet own myself. My goal is to never stop learning and understanding keywords. As I grow to understand these things more and more, I know I have more to offer my teams, my friends, and my family. I know that, as my treasury of words grows, I continue to grow and develop as a person, a family man, a coach, and a leader.

ABOUT THE
AUTHORS

MIKE KRZYZEWSKI is the *New York Times* bestselling
author of *Leading with the Heart: Coach K's Successful
Strategies for Basketball, Business, and Life.* He has
been the head basketball coach at Duke University
since the 1980–81 season, leading the Blue Devils
to ten Atlantic Coast Conference championships,
ten Final Fours, and three NCAA National Championships in 1991, 1992, and 2001. He was inducted
into the Naismith Basketball Hall of Fame in 2001.
In addition to his duties with Duke Basketball,
Krzyzewski will also serve as head coach of the USA
Men's National Team that will compete in the 2008
Olympics. Coach K is an executive-in-residence at
Duke's Fuqua School of Business and the Coach K
Center for Leadership & Ethics.

JAMIE K. SPATOLA grew up in Durham, North Carolina, and graduated from Duke University with a
BA in English in 2003. She currently resides in Law-
ton, Oklahoma, with her husband, Chris, who is a
captain in the United States Army. Jamie is the
proud daughter of Mike and Mickie Krzyzewski.